Sharing the GIFT

Resources Book for passing on Christian Meditation

Published by Meditatio
in association with Medio Media

Medio
Media

© 2013 The World Community for Christian Meditation
All rights reserved.

CONTENTS

ACKNOWLEDGEMENTS

The teaching of John Main OSB and Laurence Freeman OSB forms the foundation of this book.

Acknowledgements and thanks are due to the participants at the first 'School for Teachers' in Florence 1997, also to those members of the Community both in the U.K. and worldwide for their preparatory work, especially Carla Cooper, Peter Ng, Eileen O'Hea, Doreen Romandini, Gregory Ryan, and Elizabeth West.

Sharing the Gift: Resources Book for passing on Christian Meditation has been compiled and edited by Kim Nataraja, Director of The School of Meditation, The World Community for Christian Meditation.

For further information on The School of Meditation please contact:
The International Coordinator
E-mail: Schoolcoordinator@wccm.org
Website: www.The SchoolofMeditation.org

INTRODUCTION

You are about to embark on sharing the teaching of meditation with others. This booklet offers you resources for this, drawn from many people's experience of introducing meditation in the Christian tradition. You will also become more aware of what our Community is called to be.

Every great teacher leaves a school behind him or her and as Christians we are in the School of Christ, learning to put on Christ as St Paul said. St Benedict left his Rule to Christians in all walks of life and called the monastery a School of the Lord's service.

John Main is the founder of a school within the greater context of the School of Christ and of Christian Prayer. Through his inspiration many find a way to get back to the essentials of the Christian experience, to the prayer of the heart, to the experience of Christ within, to the indwelling Spirit. John Main knew as well as anyone that the teaching of meditation is 'caught' rather than 'taught' and yet he warmly encouraged people to work hard to pass it on, to teach it, to share it with others, whether in small groups, one-to-one, or just by their silent example. He understood very clearly that it is a personal communication and that each of us meditates because at some point in our life we had this gift communicated to us personally. Like any gift from the Spirit it demands to be shared.

Learning is always about learning to learn and in a spiritual school, above all, the teachers are students and the students are teachers. Ideal teachers are people who have enough humility, enough past experience, enough knowledge and learning to be able to go into a situation and really be open to the present moment. With any group you are with you are in a quite unique relationship. Whether you are giving a talk for an evening or for a day, you are in a very close relationship with your audience. They are listening to you and it may be a bit frightening, it may make you nervous, but you can turn that nervousness to your advantage by showing it to the audience, not trying to hide it, and finding in that weakness the sense of the Spirit. You will learn something from this experience of vulnerability. It is, to some degree, like going on stage. An actor who is going to play Hamlet six nights a week, probably feels he knows the lines but at the same time, his performance will be quite different each night, a different audience, a different place perhaps, etc. The play that he is performing has infinite meaning and ramifications that one can always learn from. But we are not acting or reading someone else's lines, in fact. We are being ourselves and speaking from our own experience within a tradition and a community.

The other thing is that if you can do that, if you can approach it in this way, (with enough preparation but also with enough spontaneity and risk) then the teaching is really enriching to you. Somehow you yourself are taught something each time. It may be something you are saying that you didn't know you knew or connection that you are making, an insight of something from Scripture. It may be a question that someone raises or just the uniqueness of that group somehow incarnates an aspect of mystery that you haven't been conscious of before.

It is important to see that the giving of the talk is a very creative work, very prayerful, a very real experience of the presence of Christ in and among all the people.

Introducing meditation to an audience of strangers takes a leap of faith; every single time we do it. As a teacher, you will find that there is no easy way through it. It takes a lot of preparation and more than a little confidence. It is always a leap of faith. If you can approach it in that way every time you give a teaching, you grow. Every act of faith deepens your own faith.

By now, you must have asked yourself why you want to teach meditation. You should want to do it. It should be something you have a hunger to do. But you should also have a healthy insecurity about it. You should want to do it but, at the same time, you should not be over-confident. On the other hand, you shouldn't feel that you don't know enough, either. There is a lot of faith, a little bit of experience, and then they cross over. You are then not quite sure, which is the faith and which is the experience. You just know that this is something you must do.

Every time that you make that leap of faith in sharing the teaching you deepen your own understanding of it. Think of it every time as a moment of innocence with the group you are with. It is certainly a moment of equality. You are with them; they are with you. There are moments in life like this: birth and death, marriages and vows of commitment, where we somehow touch in together as human beings to a primal innocence. This is what sharing a spiritual path is like. This School experience that you are about to undertake will help you to travel further along your spiritual path. Approach the School with joy, anticipation, and as one of those moments of grace and innocence.

Laurence Freeman OSB

THE TWO DOVES

The Symbol of
The World Community for Christian Meditation

The symbol of the two doves perched on the rim of a chalice or other vessel is of great antiquity and has deep resonance in many cultures.

The World Community's use of the symbol is inspired by the fifth century mosaic in Galla Placidia, one of the early Christian Churches of Ravenna, which was originally built as an imperial tomb. There are antecedents of the symbol in both Roman and Greek art but its earliest roots are probably Phoenician.

The symbol of the drinking dove is archetypal. It is a transcultural metaphor for the sacred, which is experienced only through personal absorption in reality. The association with water in Christian iconography evokes the mystical symbolism of death, birth and regeneration or purification through baptism. Water is the ancient feminine principle in nature associated with the phases of the moon and of all life-giving power. As nectar, it was the Greek symbol of immortality, as wine it becomes the blood of Christ in Christian iconography.

The dove is a Christian symbol of the Holy Spirit. In Greek mythology it was the bird of Venus, the bird of love. In Christian art, the seven gifts of the Holy Spirit came to be represented as doves perched in the Tree of Life or drinking the waters of wisdom and eternal life.

The chalice evokes the mystery of sacrifice, which is at the heart of the Christian Eucharist where the Son offers himself to the Father in the love of the Holy Spirit and unites all creation in his oblation. A striking echo of this rich spiritual symbol is found in the Mundaka Upanishad of Indian tradition that describes:

> "The birds, two sweet friends, who dwell on the selfsame tree. The one eats the fruit thereof and the other looks on in silence. The first is the human soul who resting on that tree, though active feels sad in its unwisdom. But beholding the power and glory of the higher spirit it becomes free from sorrow."

Here the dualism of the two birds suggests the underlying unity of the active and the contemplative lives of each human being. Martha and Mary are inseparable sisters in the life of all who worship God in the depth of their spirit. As John Main said:

> There is an essential harmony between Being and Action. God is pure activity. Pure stillness is not inactive. It is harmonized energy that has reached its highest and destined goal, and in this harmony the power and meaning of all movement is contained. Meditation is the realization of Being, of pure action. It cannot be a merely passive state because what is both energetic and still is, at the highest point of action, energy incandescent consciousness.
>
> *John Main*

Sharing
the GIFT

MEDITATION
in the Christian Tradition

THE WHEEL OF PRAYER

STILLNESS AT THE CENTER

The purpose of a wheel is to move a cart. Prayer is the wheel that moves our life spiritually towards God.

To turn, the wheel must make contact with the ground. If the wheel does not touch the ground, it cannot move the cart; the wheel will just spin. So there must be a real time and place in our daily life that we give to prayer.

The spokes of the wheel are like the different forms of prayer. All forms of prayer are valid and effective. We have the Eucharist, intercessory prayer, the sacraments, the reading of Scripture and personal devotions.

What holds the spokes together and turn the wheel is the hub. The spokes converge at the hub. We can think of the hub as the Prayer of Christ dwelling in our hearts.

At the hub of the wheel, there is stillness. Without the still point at the center, the wheel cannot turn.

Meditation is coming to stillness at the center of our being. When we meditate, we come into that central stillness which is the source of all our action, our movement towards God through Christ within us. The movement of the wheel requires stillness at the center. This is the relationship between action and contemplation.

WHAT IS PRAYER?

A very old definition of prayer described it as the raising of the heart and mind to God. What is the "mind"? What is the "heart"? The mind is what thinks – it questions, plans, worries, fantasizes. The heart is what knows – it loves. The mind is the organ of knowledge, the heart, the organ of love. Mental consciousness must eventually give way and open up to the fuller way of knowing which is heart consciousness. Love is complete knowledge.

Most of our training in prayer, however, is limited to the mind. We were taught as children to say our prayers, to ask God for what others or we need. But this is only half of the mystery of prayer.

The other half is the prayer of the heart where we are not thinking of God or talking to him or asking for anything. We are simply being with God who is in us in the Holy Spirit whom Jesus has given us. The Holy Spirit is the love, the relationship of love that flows between Father and Son. It is this Spirit Jesus has breathed into every human heart. Meditation, then, is the prayer of the heart uniting us with the human consciousness of Jesus in the Spirit. "We do not even know how to pray but the Spirit himself prays within us." (Romans 8:26)

For mental prayer – praying in words or using thoughts about God – we can make rules. There are many "methods of mental prayer," but for the prayer of the heart there is no technique, no rules: "Where the Spirit is, there is liberty" (2 Corinthians 3:17)

The Holy Spirit in the modern Church, especially since the Vatican Council in the early 1960's, has been teaching us to recover this other dimension of our prayer. The Council documents on the Church and the liturgy both emphasized the need to develop "a contemplative orientation" in the spiritual life of Christians today. All are called to the fullness of the experience of Christ, whatever their way of life.

This means that we must move beyond the level of mental prayer: talking to God, thinking about God, asking God for our needs. We must go to the depths, to where the spirit of Jesus himself is praying in our hearts, in the deep silence of his union with our Father in the Holy Spirit.

Contemplative prayer is not the privilege of monks and nuns or special mystical types. It is a dimension of prayer to which we are all called. It is not about extraordinary experiences or altered states of consciousness. It is what Thomas Aquinas called the 'simple enjoyment of the truth'. William Blake spoke of the need to 'cleanse the doors of perception' so that we can see everything as it truly is – infinite.

This is all about the contemplative consciousness as lived in ordinary life. Meditation leads us to this and it is part of the whole mystery of prayer in the life of any person who is seeking fullness of being.

Think of prayer as a great wheel: The wheel turns our whole life towards God. Prayer is an essential part of a fully human life. If we do not pray, we are only half-alive and our faith is only half-developed.

The spokes of the wheel represent the different types of prayer. We pray in different ways, at different times, and according to how we feel. Different people have preferred different ways of prayer. The spokes represent, for example, the Eucharist, the other sacraments, spiritual prayer, petitionary and intercessory prayer, charismatic prayer, devotions, the rosary, etc.

But what makes all these different forms of prayer Christian is that they are centered in Christ. The spokes are the forms or expressions of prayer, which fit into the hub of the wheel that is the prayer of Jesus himself.

His prayer is the essential meaning and source of a Christian's prayer. St Paul said, "I pray no longer but Christ prays in me." So, in this model of the wheel, all forms of prayer flow into and out of the spirit of Jesus worshipping God in and on behalf of creation. All forms of prayer are valid. All are effective. They are informed by the prayer of the human consciousness of Jesus that is in us by the grace of the Holy Spirit.

This is a faith understanding of the wheel of prayer. We are not thinking about all this at the time of meditation itself. Experientially, the wheel teaches us something of great importance as well. At the hub of the wheel, at the center of prayer, you find stillness. Without stillness at the center, there could be no movement or growth at the circumference. Meditation is the work of finding and becoming one with this stillness, which is the hallmark of the Spirit. "Be still and know that I am God!"

Contemplative prayer is total openness to and oneness with the prayer of Jesus. Contemplation is being silent, still and simple. And the heart of the prayer of Jesus is his communion of love with the Father, his turning his attention to the Father, in the Holy Spirit. Christian prayer, therefore, means entering the life of the Holy Trinity in, through and with the human mind and heart of Jesus.

For many people, prayer is basically an appeal to God for special help in particular times of distress. It is natural to express our faith and trust in God this way and at such times. But what is our faith in God? Is it not that, as Jesus says, God knows our needs before we ask? We do not express our needs to God either to inform God of what he does not know or to persuade God to change his mind. If we do pray for our needs, it is above all because doing so deepens our trust that God knows and God cares.

Unless this faith is clear and deep, our prayer can easily be bogged down in an arrested stage of development, stuck at the level of the ego. For many Christians this is the crisis of their faith today, and it reflects the often-shallow level of Christian spirituality.

The prayer of the heart, contemplative prayer, meditation, is essentially the prayer of faith. In silence we accept that God knows our needs and that this knowledge is the love which creates and will eventually complete us.

Adapted and summarised from Laurence Freeman OSB
Christian Meditation: Your Daily Practice

Think of prayer as a great wheel:

The wheel turns our whole life towards God. Prayer is an essential part of a fully human life. If we do not pray we are only half alive and our faith is only half developed.

The spokes of the wheel represent the different types of prayer. We pray in different ways at different times and according to how we feel. Different people have preferred ways of prayer. The spokes represent, for example, the Eucharist, the other sacraments, scriptural prayer, petitionary and intercessory prayer, charismatic prayer, devotions, the rosary, etc.

But what makes all these different forms of prayer Christian is that they are centered in Christ. The spokes are the forms or expressions of prayer which fit into the hub of the wheel which is the prayer of Jesus himself.

Laurence Freeman
Christian Meditation: Your Daily Practice

THE ESSENTIAL TEACHING

St. Paul said that we do not know how to pray, but the Spirit prays within us (Romans 8:26). This is the key to understanding the real meaning of Christian prayer. It suggests that we learn to pray not by trying to pray, but by giving up, or letting go, of our trying. And instead, learning to be.

This opens access to the deeper prayer of the heart, where we can find the "love of God flooding our inmost heart through the Holy Spirit he has given us" (Romans 6:5). This is pure experience, beyond thought, dogma and imagination.

Meditation is a universal spiritual practice, which guides us into this state of prayer, into the prayer of Christ. It brings us to silence, stillness and simplicity.

As Christians, we meditate because we believe in the Risen Christ, that he lives, and lives in us. As disciples of Jesus, the teacher, we have faith when he calls us to leave self behind and follow him into the Kingdom of God, to "share in the very being of God."

Meditation is therefore about being in relationship with Jesus; it is centered in the human consciousness of Jesus in our inmost being. Jesus knew he was both from and of the Father. This self-knowledge of Jesus is what leads us to knowing ourselves as temples of the Holy Spirit. We realize, too, that we do not have to go looking for Jesus, since Jesus has already found us. We do not choose, we are chosen. It is our faith therefore that makes our meditation Christian.

As Christians, we naturally meditate with other Christians, and our lives are guided and enriched in community by Scripture, sacrament and all the different ways of ministering to others in the love and compassion of the Spirit.

The basic theology of meditation is the basic theology of the gospel. Jesus, by his life, death and resurrection, has opened up for us a way to God, and by sending the Holy Spirit to us he has become our way and our guide.

The practice of meditation is a way to experience the gospel, not just to read it or think it. In meditation we are seeking the treasure within and we need to be prepared to leave everything in order to find it. It is the "treasure hidden in the field" spoken of by Jesus in the parable of the Kingdom. As teachers of meditation, we are called to live the experience of Jesus in our own lives, in our own journeys, and to help pass that tradition to others.

We know that meditation is very much a way of surrender, not only of images and concepts, but also of expectations. It is not a way of trying to accomplish something, of wanting to get somewhere, or of twisting God's arm, as it were. "Not my will be done, but thine be done." Meditation is about realizing, rather than acquiring. Realizing the indwelling presence of God, realizing what has already been achieved, as Father John used to say. It is about letting go of goals.

Jesus did not teach any particular method of prayer, but we can see by what he says of prayer in the Sermon on the Mount, that meditation is a way to find him and to follow him. Meditation is wholly consistent with his teaching on prayer.

- Prayer, like good works, must not be merely outward. It is not about looking holy or winning other people's admiration. Nor is it even about feeling we are holy. Jesus says your "left hand must not know what your right hand is doing." Prayer is a humble and unselfconscious work that helps us to discern reality (Matthew 6:1–4).

- Prayer must be interior. People who like their prayer to be too public easily fall into hypocrisy, which is discord between our inner and outer identity. Jesus tells us to go to "your private room" and pray in that "secret place." The word 'secret' here also means 'mysterious'. Mystery is not magic. It is the experience of reality which mental consciousness by itself cannot contain or understand. Prayer is by nature mysterious, and the deepest place of mystery in human life is the heart. The "private room" is a metaphor for the inner chamber of the heart (Matthew 6:5–6).

- In prayer we must not "babble on." More words do not make God hear us better. Prayer is not about quantity – but about quality. (Matthew 6: 7–8).

- Prayer is not primarily about asking God for things, because he "knows what we need before we ask him" (Matthew 6:8).

- We must give priority to the spiritual treasures of the Kingdom rather than material well being (Matthew 6:19–21).

- We must learn to stop worrying about the future and trust in God. Anxiety is an enemy of prayer. It makes us too self-centered and prevents us from realizing the gift already deposited in love in our heart (Matthew 6:25–37). Moreover, by telling us not to worry about tomorrow, he also asks us to stop thinking of the past and future and learn to live fully in the present moment.

- Finally, Jesus says prayer is about "setting your mind on God's Kingdom first." In other words, be attentive to the "one thing necessary" – be mindful. Then all the other things will come to you as well (Matthew 6:33).

These seven teachings of Jesus on prayer are what we put into practice in meditation: humility, interiority, silence, trust, spirituality, peace and attention.

We do not have to master any difficult techniques or theories in order to meditate. We have only to be at home and to wake up. This is what the mantra helps us to do.

Adapted and summarized from Laurence Freeman
Christian meditation: Your Daily Practice

The other-centeredness of the awakened Christian is not, strictly speaking, just the condition for prayer. It is essentially the condition of prayer, the state of prayer itself. It will always be accompanied by a personal commitment to the daily experience of prayer as a total turning of the whole person towards God, aside from all distraction and all activity, everything that is not concentrated solely upon God. Such a Christian is fulfilling St Paul's injunction to pray without ceasing' because the inner eye of his or her consciousness has been opened by redemptive contact with Christ's love and is permanently attentive to his indwelling presence. Thus every Christian is called to be a person of prayer.

John Main
Community of Love

WHAT IS MEDITATION?

Meditation, John Main taught, is a way of self-knowledge and self-acceptance. This is the indispensable first step towards any knowledge of God. But it is not primarily an intellectual knowledge, for it is reached through a profound harmony of stillness in mind and body. The body itself is part of the journey to God. Nor is it an isolated or lonely journey. The solitude of meditation awakens us to our deep interdependence with other people and so "meditation creates community".

John Main saw the Church of the future as Community. The spiritual renewal of Christianity is the next great step in its movement from medieval to modern identity. With this there will come a new appreciation of the basic Christian understanding of prayer itself. Prayer is not talking or thinking about God but being with God. My prayer is not basically mine at all if I am transcending my narrow egocentric view of reality. The essence of Christian prayer is the human consciousness of Jesus worshipping God in the Spirit at the center of the human person.

In meditation, our way forward to this growing awareness of the Spirit praying within us lies simply in our deepening fidelity to the saying of the mantra. It is the faithful repetition of our word that integrates our whole being. It does so because it brings us to the silence, the concentration, the necessary level of consciousness that enables us to open our mind and heart to the work of love of God in the depth of our being.

In starting to meditate, we have three preliminary aims. The first is simply to say the mantra for the full duration of the meditation. It will probably take some time to achieve this first stage and we have to learn patience in the meantime. We cannot force anything to happen, but must simply say the mantra without haste, or expectation.

The second aim is to say the mantra throughout the meditation without interruption, while remaining quite calm in the face of distractions. In this phase the mantra resembles a plough that continues resolutely across the rough field of our mind, undeflected by any obtrusion or disturbance.

And the third of these preliminary aims is to say the mantra for the entire time of the meditation, quite free of all distractions. The surface areas of the mind are now in tune with the deep peacefulness at the core of our being. The same harmonic sounds throughout our being. In this state we have passed beyond thought, beyond imagination, and beyond all images. We simply rest with the Reality, the realized presence of God Himself dwelling within our hearts.

This transformation of our nature is put before us as a real and an immediate possibility. The mantra is simply the devise that leads us to this central Christian experience, leading us to know from our own experience that God's love has flooded our inmost heart through the Holy Spirit. We have to prepare our hearts to receive the wonderful message of the Gospel in all its fullness. And until we have expanded our consciousness, we will be incapable of this, and will be incapable too of knowing what the traditional religious language we use really means. Meditation is precisely the way we need to follow in order to expand our hearts, broaden our vision and clarify our minds and perception. The stages of our progress in meditation will come about in their own time, God's own time. We only hinder this progression by becoming too self-conscious about our stage of development. The greatest temptation of all is to complicate the process and ourselves. "Unless you become like little children" Meditation simplifies us to the point where we can receive the fullness of truth and the fullness of love.

Adapted and summarized from John Main
Word into Silence

> It is our conviction that the central message of the New Testament is that there is really only one prayer and that this prayer is the prayer of Christ. It is a prayer that continues in our hearts day and night. I can describe it only as the stream of love that flows constantly between Jesus and his Father. This stream of love is the Holy Spirit.
>
> *John Main*
> *Moment of Christ*

THE PRACTICE

Meditation is experiential. That is, it is a way of experience not of theory or of thought at all. It is an incarnate way of prayer. The body is not a barrier between God and us. It is the sacrament of our being that God has given us. That is why the body needs to be part of the whole experience of prayer. The simple rules are:

- *Sit down: the body is relaxed but not in a position for sleep.*

- *Sit still: the body expresses the whole person's attitude of attention and reverence.*

- *Keep your back straight: the body is alert and wakeful.*

- *Breathe normally: ideally from the belly.*

- *Be relaxed but alert: the formula for peace.*

- *Gently close your eyes and begin to recite your mantra: Ma-ra-na-tha.*

- *Repeat your prayer-word throughout the time of your meditation.*

When you first sit to meditate, take a while to find a posture you can be comfortable and steady in. Relax the obvious tensions of your body, in your shoulders, neck, eyes and forehead. The basic sitting postures to try out are on a chair with a straight back, on a prayer stool, or sitting cross-legged on the floor with a small cushion beneath for support.

Choose a quiet time and place where you are not likely to be disturbed. Treat your meditation times as priority times. You will come to see why meditators regard these times as the most important times of their day. If possible keep the same time and place each day as this helps deepen the rhythm of prayer in life. Above all be gentle with yourself. Take your time to insert this new discipline into your life.

Prepare for and conclude each meditation with some music or in any way that calms and focuses you. Meditation can of course be integrated into other forms of prayer, such as the Eucharist or Scripture.

Meditation with a group each week is a powerful means of deepening and supporting the practice. Groups enable people to share each other's inspiration and encouragement and they provide an important opportunity to listen to the teaching each week. In a group the dimension of the presence of Christ which is revealed "where two or three are gathered in my name" (Matthew 18:20), is experienced.

The great practical difficulty all people find in meditation is the incessant problem of distraction. These are simply the effects of constant mental activity. The mantra is a simple and effective way to deal with all types of distraction. In the face of distraction:

- *Do not try to fight them off, whether thoughts or images or feelings.*

- *Give all your attention to the mantra, gently and faithfully returning to it all the way through your time of meditation.*

- *Pay no attention to the distractions. Treat them like background noise.*

- *Be humble, patient, faithful, and keep your sense of humor. Don't make a dark night out of every cloud. But do not underestimate the perseverance you will need or the grace you will be given.*

The mantra is like a path through a thick jungle. However narrow the path may be, follow it faithfully and it will lead you out of the jungle of the mind into the great open space of the heart. Whenever you find you have wandered off the path, simply return to it at once. Failure and success are not relevant terms to describe your experience of meditation. They are ego terms, and in meditation we are learning to "leave self, the ego, behind."

Adapted and summarized from Laurence Freeman
Christian Meditation – Your Daily Practice

> Let me remind you again of the necessity for faithfulness, in particular for the daily faithfulness to your meditation, whatever the difficulties (and they are often considerable); and your faithfulness, too, during the time of meditation to the recitation of the mantra. It is this simplicity, this faithfulness, that leads us directly into the fullness of the mystery which is the mystery of our own destiny, the mystery of the self-revelation of God and the mystery of the love of God in Jesus.
>
> *John Main*
> *The Heart of Creation*

Biblical support for
CHRISTIAN MEDITATION
from a PRESBYTERIAN point of view

I.

First, listen to this quotation from Father John Main, a Benedictine monk who recovered for our time the ancient practice of praying with a single word or phrase first used in the Christian tradition of the Desert Fathers of the third and fourth centuries.

> "Christian meditation is the process in which we take time to become aware of our infinite potential in the context of the Christ-event."

He went on to say in his *Moment of Christ*:

> "Basically, meditation is a way of coming to your own center, the foundation of your own being, and remaining there-still, silent, attentive ... Meditation is in essence a way of learning to become awake, fully alive and yet still. ... It is the stillness of meditation that leads you forward to the state of wakefulness and the sense of being completely alive that dawns in you because you are in harmony with the whole of creation. The experience of meditation puts you in resonance with all life. But the way to that resonance ... that wakefulness is silence and stillness."

In other writings John Main places great emphasis upon *poverty of spirit* as a required state of mind for the meditator. Thus we have a list of key words or concepts or essential attitudes of Christian Meditation as taught by John Main. As I have suggested in the foregoing, they are *silence, stillness, attention, wakefulness, poverty of spirit*.

One of these words is found in the Hebrew Scriptures in I Kings:19 in the story of Elijah's disastrous competition with the prophets of Baal. Elijah has won the competition to discover whose god is strongest or greatest: Yahweh or Baal. Things take a bad turn when Elijah decides that he and his supporters must kill all the prophets of Baal, which they proceed to do. Then he receives the inevitable message from Queen Jezebel, which throws him into a panic: "The gods will get you for this and I'll get even with you! By this time tomorrow you'll be as dead as any one of those prophets." Elijah did what we would have done – he ran for dear life far into the desert of south Judah, wanting only to die, to be done with it all.

As the story goes, the angel of God let him rest there under a shady bush and gave him bread and water until he regained his strength. After his rest, he walked and walked all the way to the mountain of God, to Horeb or Mt. Sinai. When he got there, he crawled into a cave and went to sleep. Then the voice of God woke him: "So Elijah, what are you doing here?" And Elijah answered, "I've been working my heart out for the Lord the God of Hosts. The people of Israel have abandoned your covenant, destroyed your places of worship, and murdered your prophets. I'm the only one left, and now they're trying to kill me." He was told to "Go stand on the mountain before God. God will pass by." The spectacle that comes to mind as we read the words of I Kings 19:11–13 is truly amazing:

> "Now there was a great wind, so strong that it was splitting mountains and breaking rocks in pieces before the Lord, but the Lord was not in the wind; and after the wind an earthquake, but the Lord was not in the earthquake; and after the earthquake a fire, but the Lord was not in the fire; and after the fire a sound of sheer silence. When Elijah heard it he wrapped his face in his mantle and went out and stood at the entrance of the cave."

It was not in the sound and fury of wind, earthquake, and fire but in the silence that God revealed God's self to Elijah. In the practice of meditation an environment of silence is very helpful in our effort to be totally present to the Spirit of God and to all that is. Silence is always helpful, but not always essential, especially as one finds oneself in situations where ambient silence is impossible to obtain, such as in a busy airport or in flight. Of course a set of ear plugs would be helpful in such situations.

Other references to silence or being silent I want to highlight are found in Zechariah and Habakkuk. Zechariah was a Hebrew prophet in the period 520 to 518 Before the Common Era and was sent to the people of Judah who had suffered so much after the fall of Jerusalem in 586. He came to them with a message of hope and comfort: "Therefore, thus says the Lord, I have returned to Jerusalem with compassion; my house shall be built in it...." (1:16) A little later, Zechariah admonishes the people, "Be silent, all people, before the Lord; for he has roused himself from his holy dwelling" (2:13) The proper attitude before God the Lord, the prophet says, is silence, and meditation demands our own silence. Another prophet, Habakkuk, sounds a similar note. He has just completed an indictment of all human tyranny and concluded with a mocking indictment of their idols of stone and wood, covered in gold and silver plate when he says, "But the Lord is in his holy temple; let all the earth keep silence before him!" (Habakkuk 2:20) Here again silence before God is an appropriate attitude, and meditation requires it. In this context, the silence required is in service to the full attention we must give to God's revelation of himself. John Main says in *Community of Love*:

> "It is only in silence and through silence that we can interiorize what is beyond our comprehension and apprehend the power of a design larger than ourselves: it is the medium of transcendence."

The second word I want to draw your attention to is found in Psalm 46. The psalmist describes a natural world whose foundations are shaking and trembling and a political world in turmoil where "nations are in an uproar, the kingdoms totter," but it is a world in which God's rule will triumph, "for the Lord of hosts is with us; the God of Jacob is our refuge." In order to know this, to experience the presence and power of God, while everything appears to be falling apart around us, the psalmist declares the word of the Lord, "Be still and know that I am God." It is in the ceasing of our frantic rushing to and fro and our pausing from the many tasks which occupy our time on any given day that we begin to experience a certain stillness that is foreign to most of us in our daily lives. But perhaps it takes the word of the present Christ commanding the turmoil of our lives to cease as when he commanded the wind and the waves on the Sea of Galilee saying, "Peace! Be still." Thus the Spirit of God is saying to us today, "Time out!" "Be still if you would know me." Hence the emphasis John Main puts upon stillness in meditation, the ceasing of all physical activity or any movement, as much as possible.

When we take into account that interior and exterior silence as well as physical and mental stillness are key components of Christian Meditation, it becomes apparent that one's whole self is addressed: body, mind and spirit. To the practitioner it is also clear that this form of prayer is sacred work and not a time of physical and mental sloth.

II.

Let's move now into the New Testament scriptures and look at Jesus' experience with prayer, his teaching regarding prayer and two stories which are instructive as we practice Christian meditation.

Christian Meditation is Christian because it is grounded in the life and work of Jesus the Christ.

Although there is, to my knowledge, no specific reference to meditation or contemplative prayer as such in the gospels, there is ample reason to infer its use. It is instructive, therefore, to consider Jesus' experience with prayer.

Recall our Lord's "40 days and 40 nights" in the wilderness at the end of which he endured the temptations of Satan (Matt. 4:1–11) The 40 days and nights are, most likely a symbolic period of time like the 40 years the Israelites spent wandering in the wilderness after their exodus from Egypt. The silence must have been intense, inescapable. What Jesus did during his time in "the wilderness", except fasting, praying and enduring temptations, no one really knows. That he fasted is part of the story and that he prayed can be assumed, as that was part of the religious observance of fasting. How he prayed out there all alone we do not know, but it is not a stretch to believe that he sat very still and silent in an attitude of patient waiting before God.

Think about it. Over a long period of time in solitary prayer, one runs out of words and begins to repeat oneself. In fact that is why I have come at last to meditation personally. Some people grow weary of always bringing their personal agenda in very repetitive form to God. Does God not know what we need even before we ask? Does God need to be instructed as to the state of the world? Do we not finally exhaust the power of speech to express the ineffable longings of our hearts? Over time are we not at last reduced to silence and simply being present before God and all that is? Thus Jesus sat in silence and stillness for long hours waiting before God in an attitude of meditation. John Main says that the prayer of Jesus is a "stream of love constantly flowing from him to the Father" which it would seem is about as good a description as possible of the kind of praying Jesus probably did in the wilderness.

In meditation we experience distractions or random thoughts, which range over an entire spectrum of things – from important to trivial – regarding our lives and the world. I've not heard others say this, but I believe it is possible that the "temptations" of Jesus in the wilderness are not literal events but are probably distractions which passed through Jesus' mind as he meditated, indeed distractions which struck at the very heart of his identity and mission as God's Anointed. Such distractions would have been profoundly intense due to his physical needs and discomforts. John Main advises us simply to let them go, not to dwell on them, but to focus our attention on the mantra.

On other occasions (Mt. 14:13–22 and Lk. 6:12) we get glimpses of Jesus at prayer: He went up the hillside to pray after feeding the multitude and sending his disciples across the Sea of Galilee. It had been a long day in a succession of long days and he needed time to be alone with his Father. Another such time is when Jesus went into the hills and prayed all night prior to calling his disciples. Praying all night is not a time for words but for waiting in silence and stillness before God. Thus it is possible, even probable that he practiced contemplative prayer or meditation, but not to the exclusion of other forms of prayer. The entire 17th chapter of the Gospel according to John is devoted to "Jesus' high priestly prayer," a lengthy prayer of supplication for himself and intercession for his disciples and all who would "believe in me through their word." The gospels according to Matthew, Mark and Luke report two more occasions of Jesus praying discursively, in Gethsemane and on his cross of crucifixion. The point I wish to stress regarding the prayer of Jesus in Gethsemane is his request of Peter, James and John that "My soul is very sorrowful, even to death; remain here and watch" as he went "a little farther" (Mark 14:34–35). Was that far enough that Jesus was out of hearing range? Were the three disciples awake long enough to hear what Jesus prayed? Left open is the possibility that the words of Jesus' prayer are a later addition and that he was silent and attuned to the stream of love flowing between himself and the Father.

Consider the teaching of Jesus on prayer (Matthew 5:5–13):

> "And when you pray, you must not be like the hypocrites; for they love to stand and pray in the synagogues and at the street corners, that they may be seen by men ... But when you pray, go into your room and shut the door and pray to your Father ..."

The sin of the hypocrite in the parable is spiritual pride, which is a paradox, for there is no room for pride in the presence of God, only humility. There is also the parable of the Pharisee and the tax collector who went into the Temple to pray (Luke 18:9–14). While the Pharisee offered a self-righteous and proud prayer to God about all his own accomplishments, the tax collector "would not even lift up his eyes to heaven, but beat his breast, saying, God, be merciful to me, a sinner!" Humility is the appropriate posture before God. Jesus also taught that prayer should be kept simple when he said, "Do not heap up empty phrases as the Gentiles do, for they think that they will be heard because of their many words Do not imitate them. Your Father knows what your needs are before you ask him" (Mt. 6:7–8). In other words, simplicity is the rule or guideline. The use of the mantra in the practice of meditation is an approach to prayer that is both simple and humble. It is the combination of simplicity and humility, which, comes closest to interpreting the "poverty of spirit" (from the first beatitude "Blessed are the poor in spirit, for theirs is the kingdom of heaven" Matthew 5:3), which John Main recommends that we adopt as we meditate. His meaning is that we must let go of all thoughts, ideas, theories, desires, feelings, and focus our whole attention on saying the mantra and being in the present moment.

Consider two stories involving Jesus and some of his followers which serve to underscore points I stressed earlier regarding attitudes or postures which are appropriate, or required, when we are addressed by the presence of God.

The story of the Transfiguration of Jesus is on point here (Matthew 17: 1–13; Mark 9:2–13; Luke 9:28–36). Peter, James and John were there with Jesus on the mountain and witnessed that mysterious, extraordinary event. When Peter blurted out his nonsensical proposal to build three booths or shelters for Jesus, Moses and Elijah, "a cloud overshadowed them, and from the cloud there came a voice, This is my Son, the Beloved, listen to him!" Giving attention to the voice and presence of God is another important aspect of Christian meditation. Being in the present moment, fully alert to Spirit's presence within us and all about us is the sort of attention we must bring to our meditation.

Consider the story of Jesus' visit with Mary and Martha in the Gospel according to Luke (10:38–42) in which Jesus emphasizes the necessity for us to cease our rushing about, our constant activity and to be still and attentive. The story suggests that the quality of our life depends on our being at peace with ourselves and others, being focused on that which is truly important and being attentive to the Spirit of Christ within us

There is a reference to prayer in St. Paul's letter to the Romans (8:26–27) that I want to call to your attention. The Apostle says, "The Spirit helps us in our weakness; for we do not know how to pray as we ought, but that very Spirit intercedes for us with sighs too deep for words. And God, who searches the heart, knows what is the mind of the Spirit, because the Spirit intercedes for the saints according to the will of God." The Holy Spirit prays for us because we do not know how to pray, and if we recognize that statement as true, then we know something of "poverty of spirit" which should confirm us in a spirit of humility. In Christian Meditation we believe that the Spirit prays in us as we meditate, and as John Main says we are drawn into the Prayer of Jesus, the constant stream of love between Jesus and the Father.

A final reference is from the letter to the Ephesians (5:14–17). "Awake, O sleeper and arise from the dead, and Christ will shine on you." It is a call to members of the church in Ephesus, and by extension, to Christians everywhere to, "Be careful then how you live, not as unwise people but as wise, making the most of the time, because the days are evil. So do not be foolish, but understand what the will of the Lord is." Christian Meditation is a discipline of wakeful, prayerful waiting before God, the Ground of being, which helps us to be alert and attentive to the voice and presence of God in our lives and times.

So we find that in the Hebrew and Christian scriptures there are repeated references to the key words, or concepts or essential attitudes of Christian Meditation as taught by John Main: Thus Christian Meditation is a discipline of silence, stillness, humility, simplicity, attention, poverty of spirit, and wakefulness which, as John Main says, "leads (us) to the sense of being completely alive that dawns in (us) because (we) are in harmony with the whole of creation. But the way to that resonance ... is silence and stillness."

Christian Meditation addresses the universal phenomenon of spiritual hunger about which Roland Rolheiser has written in his book, *The Holy Longing*:

"This contemplative approach to prayer, we believe, is at least a large part of the answer to the widespread hunger or search which is present within the worldwide community of faith and among the disaffected members of the churches."

Sharing *the* GIFT

The Way of the MANTRA

THE MANTRA in the
Christian Tradition of Meditation and the
Teaching of John Main

The teaching on the mantra is the heart of John Main's teaching on prayer. It is also his most important contribution to contemporary Christian spirituality with ramifications into many aspects of the church and its place in the modern world. It is therefore important to know clearly what he taught and how this teaching relates to the entire Christian tradition of prayer both in the way it derives from that tradition and contributes to its development.

What he came to teach grew out of his own experience of the spiritual journey and his own life story.

JOHN MAIN'S DISCOVERY AND REDISCOVERY OF THE MANTRA

In *The Gethsemani Talks*, John Main describes how he first encountered the mantra and began to practice meditation. His Indian teacher, Swami Satyananda, responded to the young Irishman's eagerness to deepen his own Christian faith and life of prayer when he introduced him to the mantra as a way of calming what he referred to as the distracted monkey-mind. John Main, in the early 1950's, also displayed an unusual openness to another religious tradition in responding to this teaching. As he tells us, this was due to the strong personal impression made upon him by his teacher as a man of God and as someone whose spiritual teaching was lived out in such active compassion and social commitment

We might see this early experience of a spiritual teacher as underlying the importance John Main later attributed to having a teacher for the journey of meditation:

> "Learning to meditate is not just a matter of mastering technique. It is much more learning to appreciate and respond directly to the depths of your own nature ... Ideally you should find a teacher who will help to guide you on your pilgrimage. This little book may inspire you to do that." (WS)[1]

For many people around the world John Main has become that teacher they were looking for – a teacher who pointed them to Christ as the

---

[1] WS abbreviation for *Word into Silence:* John Main

teacher of all. Nearly thirty years after he met his own teacher in Malaysia, and shortly before his own death, he spoke about the essential advice on meditation he had received. This he said, was the best advice he had ever been given about prayer and it could be summed up in three words: Say your mantra.

The repetition of a single word or short phrase to still the mind and open the heart did not seem wholly foreign to John Main when he first heard of it. A great deal of Christian prayer in its many forms, devotional and liturgical, involves the repetition, often in a chant-like way, of the same words: the rosary, the litany, even the prayer of the Divine Office or the Eucharist. Typical Christian mantras are the Our Father, Hail Mary, and Glory Be. Although the western tradition does not have the elaborate and sophisticated 'science of the mantra' found in the east, the practice itself is well established.

What was new to the young John Main was the simplicity and precision of his teacher's exposition on the mantra. Elaborate thoughts or feelings are abandoned in the practice of the mantra that is concerned not with the activities of the mind but in opening up the treasures of the heart.

John Main did not maintain contact with his teacher (who died at an early age in 1961), but he persevered in his daily meditation that became the foundation of his spiritual life. When he was told to give it up by his novice master in 1958, he reluctantly returned to a largely exclusive routine of mental, vocal and liturgical prayer. But after some years, his reading of the 17th century English Benedictine monk Augustine Baker served to reintroduce him to his practice of meditation. Baker held a revered place in Benedictine spirituality. His emphasis on the contemplative life, his conviction that this was the way to spiritual maturity, his insistence that the path was open to lay and monastic people alike and his insight into the efficacy of mantra-like aspirations and ejaculatory prayer all caught John Main's attention at a crucial moment in his own life.

Above all Baker sent John Main to John Cassian. There in the Ninth and Tenth Conferences on Prayer he found the Christian tradition of the mantra described with clarity and confidence. Cassian, like the other masters in the Desert Tradition, was concerned with achieving the goal of the monk's life – continuous prayer – and in coping with the perennial problem of mental distractions. He recommended the continuous, 'ceaseless', repetition of a formula by which the monk would be led into 'pure prayer' or the 'prayer of fire' and to deeper union with the Risen Christ. In addition, the mysteries of Holy Scripture would be understood and tasted with incomparably greater intensity. Cassian's key to this prayer of the heart that dealt effectively with the overwhelming problem of distractions was the first of the Beatitudes – poverty of spirit.

Following this thread John Main found the same essential teaching on the mantra in the hesychast tradition of the Jesus Prayer, the fourteenth century *Cloud of Unknowing* and in modern masters like Abbot John Chapman.

The tradition of Christian meditation is very simple and above all a practical response to this question of how to pray at depth; and yet within it is concentrated the rich and profound experience of the saints known and unknown (WS, x).

John Main thus began to meditate again. At first his thoughts about how this tradition could enrich the Church were limited to the monastic life. But soon he realized that the relevance of this 'very simple device' was really to be found in the way it met the crying need of so many people of all ages and walks of life for a deeper experience of prayer.

His first published teachings on meditation were in response to the appeal of active missionaries for ongoing support. His principle way of teaching, however, always remained oral and personal. Above all, he would not talk about meditation in the abstract. The mantra, he would say, is caught not taught. If he spoke about it he would always meditate with his listeners.

The profoundest teaching and the end of all the words will be a participation in the creative moment of prayer (WS, xi).

> "Basically your teacher has only one instruction to give you and that is to say your mantra. More than this is simply encouragement and comfort until the mantra is rooted in your consciousness."

HOW TO SAY THE MANTRA

> "Lovingly and in a deep spirit of faith." (WS, 17)

Without haste or expectation. There is no prescribed method for saying it except it should be said interiorly, silently and in physical stillness without movement of lips or tongue. The syllables should be articulated clearly. Many people co-ordinate the mantra with the breath but no particular breathing technique is recommended. A frequent approach is to say the mantra on the in-breath and to breathe out in silence. Attention should be focused on the sound of the mantra. You should 'listen to it'. Say it gently and faithfully without too much effort. Do not use it as a tool to repress or drive thoughts away. Ignore all distractions. (All thoughts and feelings during meditation are distractions.) Do not analyze the meaning of the mantra. Embrace it generously as a discipline.

"Meditation is not a technique of prayer ... I say simple not easy ... The way of simplicity soon becomes a pilgrimage in which we will experience the difficulty of laying down our lives ... The fruit of the radical simplicity of the mantra is a joy beyond description and a peace beyond understanding" (*Word into Silence*).

The Cloud advises to say the word 'whole and entire' and ceaselessly. Cassian says that the mantra embraces all our thoughts and feelings so that we can 'renounce all the riches of thought and imagination'.

METAPHORS

John Main uses a variety of symbols to describe the mantra including: a harmonic, a plough, a radar bleep, polishing a mirror, a journey, a plectrum, a pilgrim's staff, a tall pole, a magnet drawn over iron filings, a key, a pendulum, a windscreen wiper. Saying it could become like toiling up a mountainside as it sounded deep in the valley below you (WS, 54).

THE DISCIPLINE AND CHOOSING THE MANTRA

Twice a day, morning and evening for a minimum of twenty minutes and for an ideal time of thirty minutes. A quiet time and place and, when possible, the same time and place each day. Sit still and upright. Stay with the same word. Do not chop and change.

Choose the mantra in consultation with a teacher. It should be a word sacred in your tradition. It helps to choose a word not in your language so that it does not have mental associations. The word we recommend is Maranatha, an ancient Aramaic prayer which means 'Come, Lord'. The sound of the word is what is important, especially the open vowel ("Ah") in 'Maranatha'. Above all, stay with the same word and keep returning to it however often distractions interrupt your attention.

The challenge of the mantra must be faced and it is not helped by constantly changing it to an 'easier' one. If and when you do need to change, the help you need, will be given to you. All we have to do is to begin – and keep on beginning.

PROCESS AND PROGRESS

Meditation is a process and it is best not to analyze both yourself and certainly not the meditation periods themselves for signs of progress. What may seem like a wasted meditation to you may be the most important of your life, John Main said. Patience and perseverance with the daily discipline are pre-eminent. However, without losing sight of the ideal, you must learn to be patient with yourself in the face of setbacks, backsliding or laziness, or indiscipline in your practice.

Gradually the mantra moves from head to heart. At first it seems as if you are saying it in your head battling all kinds of distractions. Imperceptibly, your attention span increases and it moves to your heart. John Main said there are three preliminary aims: first to say the mantra for the full duration of the meditation (give it 25 years), then to say it while remaining calm in the face of distractions, and finally to say it free from all distractions beyond thought and imagination.

Another way of describing the process is to say that at first you say the mantra, then you sound it and finally you listen to it.

> "It is at this moment that our meditation is really beginning. We are really beginning to concentrate away from ourselves ... wrapped in ever-deepening attention." (WS,54)

WHAT DOES THE MANTRA DO?

Deepening fidelity to the mantra leads to a growing awareness of the divine presence within us. An integration and simplification of the whole being unfolds by opening us to the work of the love of God in the depth of our being.

The mantra allows us to 'leave self behind' in a fundamental response to the call of Jesus to follow him into his paschal mystery. Every meditation is a model of that life cycle of death and resurrection. We take the attention off ourselves. We stop thinking about ourselves. Thus we become (as we are created to be) other-centered and more loving. Our consciousness finds a deeper and more authentic center. It unhooks us little by little from ego-consciousness. The mantra brings the mind to stillness, silence and concentration.

The fruits of meditation are felt in daily life, especially in our relationships. The fruits of the spirit (Gal 5) become more evident as the unfolding of the divine life through our human nature. This, above all, shows that the saying of the mantra is an act of faith and love. Life's values and priorities change naturally and become more harmonized with the spirit.

We grow more silent in that we become more attentive, to God and to others. An alert stillness in mind and heart transforms life as we are led from 'depth to depth of purifying silence' (WS, 31). This silence is not just ours but the silence of Christ:

> "There in the silence of the Word we share his experience of hearing Himself eternally spoken by the Father." (WS, 34)

SAYING THE MANTRA CONTINUOUSLY

This is the heart of John Main's teaching and of his transmission of the tradition of the mantra. He quotes Cassian's warning against the 'pax perniciosa' (pernicious peace) and 'sopor letalis' (lethal sleep) as the holy floating in which we can waste many years or an entire lifetime.

A particularly dangerous moment is when the mantra leads us into a state of repose and peace. We think we have no thoughts, not realizing that itself is a thought. We try to hold on to the experience of peace without seeing that to try to possess a gift brings about its loss.

> "The simplicity of the continuous repetition of the mantra means we avoid these obvious kinds of self-deception, which so easily put the ego back in charge of 'my' prayer. The call of meditation is to total poverty of spirit. It is simple but not easy." (WS, 56)

FOREVER?

In *Word into Silence*, 55 and at slightly more length in the introduction to one of his last writings, *Moment of Christ*, John Main succinctly describes how the mantra may, probably after long practice, lead you (at times) into absolute silence. This experience should not be sought or fabricated.

It was not John Main's approach to teaching to describe these experiences because he realized that not only are they indescribable but that trying to imagine them before you have had them can be severely counter-productive to your progress. So it is important to say the mantra until you can no longer say it and as soon as you realize you have stopped saying it start saying it again.

THEOLOGY

John Main was too good a theologian and too practiced in other forms of prayer to say that the mantra was 'the only way'. He did say honestly:

> "It is the only way I have found. In my own experience it is the way of pure simplicity that enables us to become fully, integrally aware of the Spirit Jesus has sent into our heart." (WS, 42)

He compares (WS,39) the mantra to the Eucharist in the way it spans levels of consciousness and dimensions of time.

> "It is our echoing response to the love-cry of the Spirit to the whole life of Jesus returning to the Father." (WS,39)

In scripture (See: *The Burning Heart*) and theology as well as in many other varied sources John Main found illustrations of the way the mantra helped the Christian to 'verify the truths of the faith in your own experience'. In *Word into Silence* he develops his theology of meditation in the light of this experience and at the service of leading others into it for themselves. He insisted that there was little point in arguing about the mantra with someone who refused to enter into the experience of silence it leads you to.

His theology is centered in the Christian vision of unity (WS, vii). He identifies the experience of God in Jesus as the universal call to holiness and contemplation and the reality that the prayer is not "my prayer but the prayer of Jesus himself," which is his return in love to the Father in his human consciousness and his return to us in the Spirit. In meditation we open our human consciousness to his and so go with him on his return to the Father in the Spirit.

The mantra allows this opening to take place through silence and poverty of spirit:

> "The mantra stills and summons all our faculties to the resolution of a single point ... complete simplicity which demands not less than everything." (WS, 44)

The all-important aim in Christian meditation is to allow God's mysterious and silent presence within us to become more and more not only a reality, but the reality in our lives; to let it become that reality which gives meaning and shape and purpose to every thing we do; to everything we are.

John Main
Word into Silence

THE WAY OF THE MANTRA

It sounds quite incredible, almost unbelievable, to us when we first begin to learn to meditate that the discipline of saying this little word, our mantra, can be a profound spiritual path that gradually transforms our life in a profound way. But it does. Think of the mustard seed that Jesus refers to in the Gospel that grows into a huge tree and the birds of the air come to rest in its branches. The mantra is just the same. It's a very small word, it's a tiny seed of faith but it does root us beyond ephemera, beyond things that are just passing away. It roots us in that eternal reality which we call God.

The mantra is an expression of our faith and love. If you like, it is a sacrament in the sense that it is an outward expression of our inner faith in the presence of God in our hearts. In our meditation, all our feelings of faith, love, devotion, praise, thanksgiving etc., are contained in the faithful and unconditional saying of the prayer word.

The saying of the mantra is the way of prayer that leads us to the condition of silence and stillness, of simplicity, of poverty of spirit, of total and selfless attention to the indwelling presence of the Holy Spirit. It is the way of silence, stillness, simplicity, commitment, discipline, poverty of spirit, of leaving self behind, of faith, of sacrifice, of generosity, and thus of love. The way "of" is also the way "to." So the way to silence is the way of silence. No wonder the faithfulness to the saying of the mantra leads to the development of these spiritual attributes in our life.

The mantra is the way that enables us to transcend the distractions and the machinations of our ego during our meditation.

Father John describes the power of the mantra in the following metaphors:

- A radar bleep leads an aircraft home through thick fog. As long as the plane is focused on this radar bleep, it knows its own course; it's homing in on its destination. The mantra is like a harmonic that we sound in the depths of our spirit, leading us home, to the source of harmony, to our center. When we listen to that harmonic sounding in our own heart, we gradually and simply come into harmony throughout our own being and so into harmony with all creation, and into harmony with God.

- The mantra is like one of those signals that keep flashing in the dark, guiding a boat to port or an aircraft to the runway. It flashes in the dark. When you begin meditating, you have to say your mantra in the dark. You have to make that act of faith.

■ The mantra is like the needle of a compass. It heads you always in the direction you must follow, away from self into God. Whichever way your ego may lead you, the compass is always faithful in the direction it points you. The mantra, if you say it with generosity, with faithfulness, and with love, will always point you in the direction of God.

■ A magnet drawn over iron fillings pulls them into their proper force fields. In the same way, the mantra rearranges us by bringing all our powers and faculties into line with each other.

■ The mantra resembles a plough that continues resolutely across the rough field of our mind, undeflected by any obstacle.

■ When we are able to sound the mantra smoothly in our hearts, it is like pushing lightly a pendulum that needs only a slight stimulus to set it swinging in a calm, steady rhythm.

■ The mantra is just like the sculptor with the large block of granite, chipping away. Each time we say the mantra, the form that God has for us is being formed. We may think ourselves as slow, even as unworthy, but we have only to be still and allow ourselves to be formed.

Fr Laurence Freeman describes the power of the mantra as follows:

■ The mantra is like a path through a thick jungle. However narrow the path may be, follow it faithfully and it will lead you out of the jungle of the mind into the great open space of the heart. Whenever you find you have wandered off the path, simply return to it straightaway. The great gift of the mantra is its immediacy. However long you have been distracted, lost in the jungle of the mind, you are never more than one step away from the path. Start saying the mantra again, and you are back on the path.

■ Some time ago, I was at a concert. As we waited for the concert to begin, I listened to the orchestra beginning to tune up. It was about the most discordant sound I've ever heard. Each instrument was playing its own way, in total disharmony. Then what happened was that the oboe, a quiet, little instrument, began to play and all the other instruments tuned in on its note. And gradually, the entire disharmony began to calm down. Then there was silence, and the concert began. It seems to me that the mantra is very much like that little oboe. In meditation, the mantra brings all the parts of our being, one by one, bit by bit, into harmony. And when we are in harmony, we are the music of God.

■ When we first begin to meditate, we are unfamiliar with a mantra such as Maranatha. If the mantra is to become familiar to us (i.e. become rooted in us), then we need to pray it as often as we can. In the time we specifically set aside for meditation, 20 or 30 minutes, we say it with all possible attention. But that period of time is not particularly lengthy and the rest of the day and night remains. The mantra can overflow into these hours. There are many opportunities during the day when we can recite the mantra and thus root it in our being a little more deeply each time. Such opportunities as washing up, cleaning a car, jogging or walking, waiting for public transport, traveling in the bus or on the commuter train, or going up many floors in an elevator. Saying the mantra silently at these times is a wonderful way of practicing the presence of God in everything we do.

■ The continuous saying of the mantra, in the midst of all our distractions at the time of our meditation, becomes an interior manifestation of our steadfast faith in God, no matter what happens in our life.

■ We all may use the same mantra, Maranatha, for our individual meditation. But it is the faith, the faithfulness, and the love that we give to it that makes it special for each one of us.

Peter Ng

"We call the prayer-word 'mantra'. This is a Sanskrit term for what John Cassian calls 'a formula of prayer' and the Cloud, 'one little word'. The term 'mantra' has now entered English usage, just as the Hebrew 'amen' or the Greek 'Christos'. Perhaps this is a sign of the vast and mysterious process by which East and West are being married today. But there is no special significance in its being an Eastern term. The advantage of using it is precisely that it does make us realize that this meditation is different from what we may think prayer to be. It is not about talking to God or thinking about God or asking for anything. The word 'maranatha' is Aramaic, Jesus' language, for 'Come, Lord'. It is one of the earliest recorded Christian prayers and was used as what we would now call a mantra."

Laurence Freeman
Light Within

THE MANTRA, DISTRACTIONS AND THE MONKEY MIND

THE ROLE OF THE MANTRA IN DEALING WITH DISTRACTIONS.

The problem all of us have in coming to an inner silence in meditation is that our minds are full of thoughts, images, sensations, emotions, insights, hopes, regrets, a never ending array of distractions.

St Teresa of Avila once said the human mind is like a boat where mutinous sailors have tied up the captain. The sailors all take a turn at steering the boat and of course the boat goes around in circles and eventually crashes on the rocks. That is our mind, says Teresa, full of thoughts taking us off in every direction. She also says:

> "Distractions and the wandering mind are part of the human condition and can no more be avoided than eating and sleeping."

The human mind has been compared to a great tree with monkeys jumping from branch to branch chattering away. Laurence Freeman, in commenting on this story, says there is a path that leads through this forest of chattering monkeys and it is the practice of reciting a mantra in our daily periods of meditation.

There is another wonderful story that illustrates the capricious human mind. In India the mind is often compared to the trunk of an elephant, restless, inquisitive and always straying. In India if you watch an elephant in a parade you will see how apt the comparison is. In Indian towns and villages, elephants are often taken in religious processions through the streets to the temple. The streets are crooked and narrow, lined on either side with fruit and vegetable stalls. Along comes the elephant with his restless trunk, and in one quick motion it grabs a whole bunch of bananas. You can almost see him asking, 'What else do you expect me to do? Here is my trunk and there are the bananas.' He just doesn't know what else to do with his trunk. Then from the next stall he picks up a coconut and tosses it in after the bananas. There is a loud crack and the elephant moves to the next stall. No threat can make this restless trunk settle down.

But the wise trainer, if he knows his elephant well, will simply give that trunk a short bamboo stick to hold on to before the procession starts. Then the elephant will walk along proudly with his head up high, holding the bamboo stick in front of him like a drum major with a baton. He is not interested in bananas or coconuts any more; his trunk has something to hold on to.

The human mind is very much like this trunk of an elephant. Most of the time it has nothing to hold on to. But it can be kept from straying into the world of thoughts, imagination and fantasy by simply giving it something to hold on to a mantra.

The mantra is help towards concentration, enabling us to go beyond distractions, including words and thoughts, even holy thoughts. We say the mantra slowly, steadily with attentiveness. When we find our mind has wandered we simply come back to our mantra. We cannot force this way of prayer through sheer will power. Do not try too hard. Let go; relax. There is no need to fight or struggle with distractions. Simply return to the repetition of the mantra.

John Main also reminds us that we cannot attempt to force the eliminations of distractions. In fact we must let go of goals and trying to achieve anything. The mantra will become rooted in our consciousness through the simple fidelity of returning to the mantra each morning and evening. Meditation is centering ourselves on our inner core and opening ourselves to Christ praying within us.

But a word of caution should be offered here. The repetition of a mantra does not bring instant peace, harmony, the absence of distractions or silence. We must accept we are on the pilgrimage of meditation. We should not get upset at continual distractions. Our aim is not to be free of all thoughts. Again this would be a goal and we do not want to have goals. John Main constantly advises us not to come to meditation with any expectations. So do not struggle or fret over distractions. The mantra simply expresses our openness to God and his indwelling presence.

Simone Weil, the French author, who died in 1943 at the age of 33, was an apostle of the spiritual life and defined prayer as attention. The mantra leads us to this attention.

Pascal felt the greatest enemy of prayer was the 'Gethsemani sleep' when the apostles slept instead of watching with Jesus. Pascal felt that inattention and drowsiness were the enemies of prayer. Again the mantra helps us with this problem by bringing us to attention.

A problem often observed by those meditating is that the thinking process continues even while saying the mantra. There is even a term for this. It is called double tracking. Again this is nothing to be concerned about. With perseverance the mantra will become stronger and our thoughts will diminish as the pilgrimage of meditation continues.

It is important to remember that when we are bombarded with thoughts and images at our time of meditation our will is still tuned in to the presence of God. To handle distractions we do require gentleness and patience. We have to wait, like the wise virgins, in patience and hope. Gentleness and patience indicates that the spirit is working silently within us.

Adapted from Paul Harris
Christian Meditation Contemplative Prayer for a New Generation

I want now to address a particular question that we all encounter. It is the question of distractions. What should you do when you begin to meditate and distracting thoughts come into your mind? The advice that the tradition has to give us is to ignore the distractions and to say your word and to keep on saying your word. Don't waste any energy in trying to furrow your brow and say, 'I will not think of what I am going to have for dinner', or 'who I'm going to see today', or 'where am I going tomorrow', or what ever the distraction may be. Don't try to use any energy to dispel the distraction. Simply ignore it and the way to ignore it is to say your word.

John Main
Moment of Christ

CHOOSING THE MANTRA

As previously mentioned, Maranatha is one of the oldest Christian prayers. It is a word in Aramaic, the language that Jesus spoke, and means 'Come, Lord Jesus' or 'The Lord Comes'. St Paul ends his first letter to the Corinthians with this word and it is the last word in St John's Book of Revelation (See: 1 Cor. 16:22; Rev. 22:20). Paul was writing to the Corinthians in Greek but at the end of his letter inserts the Aramaic word Maranatha. Scripture scholars tell us Paul was able to do this because all the early Christians fully understood this word. It was a password that allowed Christians into homes for the celebration of the Eucharist.

Maranatha also appears in one of the oldest written liturgical fragments of the Eucharist that exists. In the invitation to receive communion the priest says:

> "Praise to the Son of David. If anyone is holy, let them come. If anyone is not holy, let him or her repent. Maranatha. Come, Lord Jesus" (Didache, 10)

While Maranatha is a sacred word to Christians, nevertheless at times of meditation one does not dwell on the meaning of the word. One wants to go beyond thoughts and images and simply rest in silence in the Lord. A mantra is not something that is magical or mysterious. It is really something very practical since it calms our minds and hearts and brings us into the presence of God.

Again, in reciting maranatha the word is broken into four equally stressed syllables: Ma-ra-na-tha. And one listens to the word as a sound as it is said gently, continuously for the full period of meditation. John Main says there may come a day when we enter the cloud of unknowing, in which there is silence, absolute silence, and we can no longer hear the mantra. This absolute silence may last for only a short period of time and then we must return to saying the mantra.

OTHER CHRISTIAN MANTRAS

John Main mentions the word Jesus used in his own prayer, 'Abba'. Like 'Maranatha' this word is also in Aramaic and means 'Father'. He also mentions the name Jesus, although he felt that the Jesus mantra had certain difficulties for some head-centered Westerners, as he felt that a mantra in the meditator's own language would inevitably start associations and hence distractions. The choice of a mantra is an important one and ideally should be sanctified by long usage. A teacher, such as John Main, also generally hands down a mantra.

Here are a few mantras for Christians suggested by a variety of Christian writers. Abba; Peace; Come, Holy Spirit; Kyrie Eleison; Christ is Risen; My Lord and My God; Veni Sancte Spiritus; O Lord, Make Haste to Help Me; God is Love.

CHANGING ONE'S MANTRA

Because we want the mantra to become rooted within us, the traditional teaching is to choose one mantra and stay with it. If we continually transplant a plant and uproot it several times, there may come a time when the roots having been disturbed simply do not root again. Some people, when they come into a difficult time with distractions in their meditation, feel it is time to change their mantra. It is part of the restlessness of our age. They try one mantra for six weeks and then try another. It simply does not work that way. Choose one mantra, stick with it, and let it become rooted deep within you.

There is a lovely story (apocryphal) about an old desert hermit with a mantra that had been rooted within him for forty years. Sometimes he liked to recite it out loud. His deep life of meditation enabled him to work minor miracles like calling down the rain from the sky, walking on water on a nearby river, and other neat things, or so the story goes. One day some visiting monks heard him chanting his mantra and felt he was not pronouncing his word correctly. So they decided fraternal correction was in order and they taught him how to pronounce it the correct way. The hermit was humble and thanked them profusely for the correct pronunciation. From that point on he said it correctly. However, the next time he went to walk on water he sank to the bottom of the river.

There is a story comparing a person who keeps changing the mantra to a farmer who digs in ten different places looking for water. The farmer starts digging in one spot until the digging becomes difficult, then goes on to another spot. In the new spot he says, 'It's too crumbly here, I'll try another spot'. Next he hits a rock and for the rest of the day goes from spot to spot. The point here is that if the farmer had spent the same amount of time and energy in digging in one place he would soon go deep enough to find water. It's the same with choosing and reciting one's mantra. Persevere and stick with one mantra and one will find living water.

Adapted from Paul Harris:
Christian Meditation, Contemplative Prayer for a New Generation

THE WAY OF THE MANTRA IN THE EASTERN AND WESTERN TRADITION OF CHRISTIANITY

"The mind should unceasingly cling to the until strengthened by continual use of it, it casts off and rejects the rich and ample matter of all kinds of thought and restricts itself to the poverty of the single verse Those who realize this poverty arrive with ease at the first of the Beatitudes; 'Blessed are they who are poor in spirit for theirs is the Kingdom of Heaven'"

John Cassian – Conference X

"The rest you will learn with the help of God, by practicing watchfulness of spirit and by keeping Jesus in your heart, for sit down in your cell and it will teach you all things."

St. Symeon, the New Theologian

"Use this little word and pray not in many words but in a little word of one syllable. Fix this word fast to your heart so that it is always there come what may. With this word, you will suppress all thoughts."

The Cloud of Unknowing – Chapter 7

"Sitting in your cell collect your mind into your heart and send out thence your mental cry to our Lord Jesus."

St. Gregory of Sinai

"So sitting down in your cell, collect your mind, lead it into the path of the breath along which the air enters in, constrain it to enter the heart together with the inhaled air, and keep it there. Keep it there, but do not leave it silent, instead give it the following prayer: 'Lord Jesus Christ, Son of God, have mercy on me'. Let this be its constant occupation, never to be abandoned it leads to Divine desire and love."

Callistos and Ignatius Philokalia

"The continuous interior Prayer of Jesus is a constant uninterrupted calling upon the divine Name of Jesus with the lips, in the spirit, in the heart. One who accustoms himself to this appeal experiences as a result so deep a consolation and so great a need to offer the prayer always, that he can no longer live without it, and it will continue to voice itself within him of its own accord."

The Way of the Pilgrim

"May the memory of Jesus be united to your breathing, and then shall you know the usefulness of silence."

St. John of the Ladder

"The very best thing one can ever do is to fix Jesus in one's heart and never want anything else."

Richard Rolle – *Fire of Love*

Simone Weil had developed the habit of reciting the Our Father in Greek:

"The effect of this practice is extraordinary and surprises me every time for, although I experience it each day, it exceeds my expectation at every recitation.

At times the very first words tear my thoughts from my body and transport it to a place outside space where there is neither perspective nor point of view. The infinity of the ordinary expanses of perception is replaced by an infinity to the second or sometimes the third degree. At the same time, filling every part of this infinity, there is silence, a silence which is not an absence of sound but which is the object of a positive sensation, more positive that that of sound. Noises, if there are any, only reach me after crossing this silence.

Sometimes, also, during this recitation or at other moments, Christ is present with me in person, but his presence is infinitely more real, more moving, more clear that on that first occasion when he took possession of me."

Simone Weil

"It is almost impossible for people starting to believe that there could be anything very significant in sitting still, closing your eyes lightly and just begin reciting a word. You have to take that on faith when you begin. I first started to meditate like this about thirty years ago. I suppose that I was as crass as anyone of my age because I was always saying to the man who taught me: 'how long is this going to take? I can't sit around here saying this word forever, you know'. He would look at me with a rather pained look, and either he would just look straight through me or else he would say, 'Say your mantra'. Thirty years later, I am still astonished at the wisdom of that teaching. As I say, you have to take it on faith when you begin. Nothing I can say will be very significant for you in comparison with the persuasive power of your own experience. You will enter into clearer and clearer simplicity."

John Main

"Father John Main always insisted that this is a very simple, humble way. 'Quietly repeating your word,' he says, 'keeps the ego in its place and should lead you to the transcendent.' But unless the mantra is accompanied by faith and love, it has no real value; it would be merely a mechanism. It is a real danger to trust the mechanism of the mantra, but as an expression of faith and love it becomes a very powerful means to direct your faith and to open you to God."

Bede Griffiths

MARANATHA

An Aramaic phrase occurring in 1 Cor 16:22. It may be turned back into Aramaic either as maran'ata, "Our Lord has come", or as marana'ta, "Come, our Lord".

The occurrence of the phrase, "Come, Lord Jesus" in Apc 22:20, which is, except for the personal name, a translation of marana'ta, makes this meaning of the phrase somewhat more probable. Paul could not have placed an Aramaic invocation in a letter to the Church at Corinth unless it were already known to them, and they could hardly have known it unless it were a well known liturgical invocation. Its origin must lie in the Palestinian communities, whence it passed into the Hellenistic churches. It is thus an attestation to the extremely early use of the title "Lord" given to Jesus. The invocation must have had its place in the celebration of the Eucharist. The "coming" for which it prays may be either the eschatological coming (cf. Parousia) or the coming in the celebration of the Eucharist. More probably the two comings should not be too sharply distinguished. The Eucharist was a messianic banquet and was a perpetual symbol and assurance of the Parousia (1 Co 11:26).

The use of the Aramaic phrase in the liturgy is parallel to the use of the Hebrew words Amen, Alleluia, and Hosanna and the Greek words Kyrie eleison in the modern Roman liturgy.

IMPORTANT PEOPLE/STAGES IN THE DEVELOPMENT OF CONTEMPLATIVE CHRISTIAN SPIRITUALITY

Ignatius of Antioch	35–107		Christocentric mystic. For him Christ's death and resurrection takes on mystical significance.
Origen of Alexandria	185–254	On Principles; Against Celsus	Great religious experience was martyrdom. Commentary on Song of Songs – spiritual betrothal most influenced development of mystical theology. He Christianised and theologised Neo Platonism. Each soul has individually fallen and must find its way back to God through the help of the logos, Christ.
St Antony	c251–356	The Letters of St Antony the Great	Early hermit or solitary monk in the desert of Egypt. Model for later monasticism particularly of the eremitical type.
St Athanasius	c296–373	Against the Gentiles; Apology Against the Arians	Bishop of Alexandria. Wrote a Life of Antony. Was an influence on later Eastern Orthodox mysticism.
Basil of Caesarea (Basil the Great)	330–379	Longer Rules; Liturgy of St Basil	Basil and Gregory of Nyssa were brothers. One of the Cappadocians and a Church Father. He gave a mystical orientation to the monastic movement.
Gregory of Nyssa	335–398	Life of Moses: Moses left everything even thinking to enter into the unknowing and meet God. Dialogue with his Sister Macrina concerning the Resurrection	Gregory along with Basil insisted on the incomprehensibility of God to the human mind and the necessary limits of theological discourse. In opposition to the Arian movement, which implied that God's being, was accessible to human intelligence. He believed that the universe existed as a harmonious order emanating from God. Attributed his spiritual development to his sister Macrina.

Gregory of Nazianzus	329–390	Orations; Forty Five Sermons	Lived in Cappadocia (now Turkey). Important in propounding Trinitarian role. Early Church Father
Council of Nicea	325		
Evagrius of Pontos	345–399		Learned Greek. Studied with the Cappadocians before going to the desert. Theology of negation. Strong influence of Origen. Spoke of "apatheia".
Augustine of Hippo	354–430	Confessions; De Trinitas	Important source for much medieval mysticism. Brings Platonism and Christianity together. He emphasises the soul's search for God, made possible by the illumination of the mind of God. Influences; Plato and Plotinus.
John Cassian	365–435	Conferences	Desert monk. Wrote of "pure prayer".
Desert Fathers and Mothers	Fourth century		
Council of Ephesus	431		
Council of Chalcedon	451		
Psuedo Dionysius	c500 ?	Concerning Mystical Theology The Divine Names The Celestial Hierarchy The Ecclesiastical Hierarchy The Letters	Extremely influential throughout the Eastern World. St Bonaventure gave him the title of "prince of mystics". Originates the distinction between apophatic spirituality (theology of negation) and kataphatic spirituality (theology of affirmation). Unknown identity.
Gregory the Great	540–604		
Dorotheus of Gaza	Fl540	Conferencias	
St John Climacus	579–649	The Ladder of Divine Ascent	Major saint in the Eastern Orthodox tradition. Also known as John of the Ladder.
John Scotus Eriugena	810–877	Periphyseon	John Scotus translated Pseudo Dionysius from Greek to Latin. He holds that humans are a microcosm of the universe. That which is shared the essence of all things is God. Influenced by Plotinus, Augustine and Pseudo Dionysius.

St Symeon the New Theologian	949–1022		Mystic who lived in the Byzantine Empire. His writings stress that the mystical experience is accessible for all those who prepare themselves to receive it.
Bernard of Clairvaux	1090–1153	Sermons; On the Love of God	Cistercian mystic. Promoted a mystical vision of rhapsodic love, in which the Church is described in erotic terms as the bride of Christ. His love mysticism has the tendency to be anti intellectual.
Victorines: Hugh of and St Victor; Richard of St Victor	1096–1142 Died 1173	On Sacraments	Hugh is the more important of the two. He argues for a close tie between reason mysticism.
Hildegard of Bingen	1098–1179	Scivias; The Book of Divine Works; Letters	Abbess of Benedictine Abbey at Bingen. Early German speculative mystic, reminiscent of Isaiah or Ezekiel at times. She was greatly respected in her time, both for her writings as well as for her music and art. Influenced by Augustine and Bernard of Clairvaux. She wrote of her mystical experiences to St Bernard and through his influence was given permission by the Pope to record them.
Beatrice of Nazareth	1200–1268	The Seven Modes of Sacred Love	Belgian Cistercian mystic. A Beguine community following the death of her mother when she was 7 educated her. At 15 she entered the Cistercian convent that her father had founded. Love is to guide one's spiritual duty. A minnemystik (Lovemystic). Love for God should be unquestioning. Reason only inhibits one's ability to love God. She employs vivid imagery such as water immersion to illustrate the power and omnipresence of God's love.
Mechtild of Magdeburg	1207–1282 (1294)	The Flowing Light of the Godhead	Strongly feminine images in mysticism. Devotional mystic. Influenced by Bernard of Clairvaux, Hildegard of Bingen, Gregory the Great. She began to have mystical experiences from the age of 12 when she believed she was "hailed" by the Holy Spirit. Joined the Beguines. Her lyrics are filled with allegorical references to such figures as Pain, Constancy and Withdrawal of God. Frequently these figure engage in spoken conversation. She was critical of the corruption in the clergy and the Dominican order. Made enemies. Fled to a Cistercian convent for protection and influenced the abbess and her younger sister – Gertrude of Hackeborn and Mechtild of Hackeborn also they lack M of M's originality. A little more concerned with avoiding sin than Beatrice of Nazareth. She falls in love with God as a would be lover.

Name	Dates	Works	Description
St Bonaventure	1221–1274	The Journey of the Mind into God; The Tree of Life; The Life of St Francis	Franciscan monk. Architect of the philosophical, theological and mystical side of Francis' thought. Mysticism in the Augustine tradition. Influenced by St Augustine, St Francis and the Victorines.
Meister Eckhart	1260–1327	Meister Eckhart: Selected Writings; Sermons; Parisian Questions; Prologues	Dominican monk. The Catholic Church repudiated Writings. One of the most important early German speculative mystics. Eckhart is the first of the so-called Rhineland mystics. Influenced by Pseudo-Dionysius.
Hadewijch of Brabant/Antwerp	Thirteenth century Died approx 1260	Letters; Poems in Stanzas; Visions; Poems in Couplets	Belgium Beguine. One of the greatest exponents of love mysticism. Influenced by Plato, Plotinus, Pseudo-Dionysius; Gregory of Nyssa, Richard of St Victor. Some regard her as the most intellectually gifted of the mystics of the thirteenth century. Her love mysticism centres on experiencing God's love. Her ultimate belief is that true and perfect love is only found by worshipping Christ. The mystic undergoes three stages of experience with love - an awareness of distance between minne [Love Itself], the complete surrender to minne and restored balance. She combines the elements of courtly love with that of mysticism to depict God as her visionary lover. New theme. Disputes the notion of a vengeful God. Her God obeys the laws of courtship, giving Hadewijch gifts and wooing her when appropriate. Thus she not only promotes the image of a loving God but also the institution of courtship itself.
John Ruysbroeck	1293–1381	The Adornment of the Spiritual Marriage; The Sparkling Stone; The Book of Supreme Truth.	Flemish mystic. Sometimes considered to be one of the Rhineland mystics. Outlines the stages of the mystical life. Influenced by Eckhart.
Henry Suso	1295–1366	A Little Book of Eternal Wisdom	A Rhineland mystic. Influenced by Eckhart.
Gregory Palamas	1296–1359		Mystical theologian and saint of the Eastern Orthodox church.
John Tauler	1300–1361	Sermons	Rhineland mystic and Dominican. Tauler emphasised the inner person rather than outer works and because of this became popular in Protestant circles in the Reformation and later Pietism and Romanticism. He was from the same community that produced the Theologia Germanica.

Name	Date	Work(s)	Description
Anonymous	1349–c1395	Theologia Germanica	Important influence in the German mystical tradition. Luther rediscovered and popularised it.
Richard Rolle	1300–1349	The Fire of Love	Part of the English "school" of late medieval mysticism. Emphasises the physicality of the mystical experience (feeling heat, seeing colours).
Bridget of Sweden	1302–1373	Revelations (Introduction, First and Second Interrogation)	Showed mystical experiences from an early age. Born into a prominent family, married and had six children. Following the death of her husband she devoted her life to religion and the practice of asceticism. Visionary and prophetess. Ascetic mystic. Heavily involved in political activity. She established a religious order (Birgittines). She spent her twenty most influential years in Rome where she healed people physically and spiritually. Influenced by St Francis of Assisi. Birgitta's Christ is described as a "Judge", but she criticises the notion of vengeance – God is full of fidelity and compassion and not of vindictiveness.
Marguerite Porete	Died 1310	Mirror of the Simple Souls	Mystic. Writings condemned in Inquisition. She asserts that the soul moves through seven stages until one reaches union with God. Influenced by the writings of Pseudo Dionysius. Two sections of the stages drew criticism from the authorities. She refused to refrain from distribution of her books. Despite support from four influential Churchmen she was burned at the stake.
Julian of Norwich	1343–1443	Revelation of Divine Love	Julian was part of the English "school" of late medieval mysticism. Mystical experience that came when she was close to death. The experience came with healing and she devoted her life to understanding her vision. Key concepts and contributions of her work include her formulation of the Trinitarian explanation of the motherhood of God, "Mother Jesus" and proving the divinity in womanhood.
Unknown English monk	Fourteenth century	Cloud of Unknowing	Part of the English "school" of late medieval mysticism. The emphasis on unknowing God is part of the Pseudo-Dionysius' apophatic theology. Influenced by Pseudo-Dionysius.
Catherine of Siena	1347–1380	Il Dialogo	Italian mystic. Advisor to Pope Gregory XI. Influenced by Augustine.
Walter Hilton	Died 1396	The Scale or Ladder of Perfection; Treatise Written to a Devout Man	An Augustinian monk. Hilton was an English mystic.

Thomas a Kempis	c1380–1471	The Imitation of Christ	Augustinian monk. Finest expression of "devotio moderna", modern spirituality, which downplays the Rhineland mystics concern with contemplation and speculative theology and stresses the practice of simple piety and asceticism. Influenced by Eckhart?
Nicholas of Cusa	1401–1464	Nicholas Cusa: Selected Spiritual Writings	German mystic. Cusa was a speculative mystic who emphasised the incomprehensibility and paradoxicality of God. Influenced by Plotinus, Pseudo-Dionysius and Eckhart.
Margery Kempe	c1430	The Book of Margery Kempe; Treatise of Contemplation	Mainly known as the biographer of Julian of Norwich.
Teresa of Avila	1515–1582	Interior Castle; The Way of Perfection; Life by T of A.	Spanish Carmelite nun. Formed the Discalced (barefoot) Carmelites with St John of the Cross. Is very important for describing the stages of the mystical journey. Influenced by Augustine.
Ignatius of Loyola	1522–1548	Spiritual Exercises	Spanish mystic. Discalced Carmelite. Both John and Teresa emphaise mysticism as
St John of the Cross	1542–1591	Ascent of Mt Carmel; Dark Night of the Soul.	union with God, attainable only in the denial of the self. Influenced by Teresa of Avila.
Jacob Boehme	1575–1624		German mystic. Lutheran. A major figure in German mysticism. Lutherans rejected his teachings. Influenced by Eckhart, Jewish Kabbalah, Valentin Weigel, Renaissance alchemy and Paracelsus.
Brother Lawrence	1611–1691	The Practice of the Presence of God	
St Francis de Sales	1567–1622	Introduction to the Devout Life	French mystic. Devout Life is a classic of French spirituality.
Quietism	1687		The book by Miguel Molinos was condemned by Pope Innocent XI in 1687
Philokalia	Eighteenth century	Philokalia	Anthology of Orthodox Spirituality compiled from texts written from the fourth to the fifteenth century.
Theophan the Recluse	1815–1894		Russian mystic
Teilhard de Chardin	1881–1955		

Ruth Fowler

Sharing *the* GIFT

The Fruits of MEDITATION

THE FRUITS OF MEDITATION

THE INTEGRATING POWER OF MEDITATION

John Main summed up the fruits of meditation like this:

> "It is my personal conviction that meditation can add a dimension of incredible richness to your life. I wish that I had the persuasive powers or the eloquence to convince everyone that I meet of the importance of meditating.
>
> Once you begin, and it takes lots of us months and years to begin, but once you begin you will find that your meditation is the great integrating power in your life, giving depth and perspective to everything you are and everything you do.
>
> And the reason for that is this: that you are beginning to live out of the power of the love of God, that power that is present in our hearts in all its immensity, in all its simplicity, in the Spirit of Jesus. The integrating power of meditation affects every part of our life. All our life is, as it were, aligned on Christ. And his life and presence makes itself felt in every part of our life. And the way to that is the way of humility, of simplicity, the way of the mantra."

THE HARVEST OF THE SPIRIT

The personal, inner change in us, as we meditate, can best be described in what St Paul called the harvest of the Spirit. (Gal 5:5)

> "Love, joy, peace, patience, kindness, goodness, fidelity, gentleness and self-control."

LOVE is placed first "the highest gift". In its path we also find a new joyfulness in life, even in times of stress and suffering.

JOY is deeper than pleasure. It is found in a new taste for the simple and natural things in life.

PEACE is the gift Jesus gave us in the Spirit. It is the energy of his own deep inner harmony with himself, with the Father, and with all creation.

PATIENCE is the cure for our bursts of irritability and intolerance, and all the ways we try to possess others.

KINDNESS is the gift of treating others, as we would like them to treat us.

GOODNESS is not "ours" but we are essentially good and our human nature is godly because we are created by God and because God lives in us.

FIDELITY is the gift that comes through the discipline of the daily meditation and the mantra. For every relationship to be human and loving, we have to deepen it with fidelity.

SELF-CONTROL is necessary if we are to enjoy life in the full liberty of the Spirit. It is the fruit of the balance of meditation, the middle way between all extremes.

In meditation, we are sanctified because we are healed. The source of our being is also the source that heals us and makes us whole. The fruits of the Spirit grow gradually in us because we begin to turn to the power of love at the center of our being.

LEARNING TO BE

We meditate to be. To be the person we are called to be. The person we are called to be is a person fully accepting the gift of our own creation, accepting and responding fully to the gift of the fullness of life given to us in Jesus. More than that we meditate as our response to our own nature as temples of the Holy Spirit. When you sit down to meditate each day, remember that the purpose of it all is to lose all self-consciousness.

Meditation helps us to be because in meditation, we learn to let go of insecurity, our images, our thoughts, and we learn to be openhearted. Meditation teaches us to respond to life without demands, without expectations.

Learning to be means:

- not wearing any "masks" to hide our real feelings; not having to act
- not responding to people in a preprogrammed way such as prejudices, the desire for attention and approval
- letting others be; letting God be

Our capacity to be, our confidence in being, comes from the experience in meditation that we are loved, loved unconditionally by God as his unique creation.

LEARNING TO LIVE FULLY IN THE PRESENT MOMENT

Meditation teaches us to be fully conscious in the present moment. This is because in meditation, we give our undivided attention to the saying of the mantra. We are fully present to the mantra, with no thoughts of the past or the future. Unless we learn to live fully in the present moment, we are living on the surface of life. The past is gone, the future is uncertain, and so all that we have is the present moment. Living a full life requires us to treasure every moment and live it consciously. This can also be described as maintaining a state of mindfulness in everything we do.

If we are living in the present moment then:

- the most important moment is NOW
- the most important person is the person you are with NOW
- the most important thing is what you are doing NOW

Fr Bede Griffiths described MINDFULNESS as follows:

> "The great spiritual teachers of all religions have themselves practiced and taught mindfulness. To be mindful is to live in the present moment, not to be imprisoned in the past, nor anticipating a future that may never happen. When we are fully aware of the present, life is transformed and the strain and stress disappear. So much of modern life is a feverish anticipation of future activity and excitement. We have to learn to step back from this into the freedom and possibility of the present."

BECOMING MORE ROOTED, MORE CENTERED

To be more rooted, more centered means to be more steady, more consistent in the way we approach life, especially problems in life. We are less flappable, less volatile. We are less likely to swing between extremes in our moods and actions. We are guided by certain core values. We develop a better understanding of:

- what is truly important in life
- what is trivial
- what is passing
- what truly endures

Meditation helps us to this rootedness and centeredness because, in the daily discipline of meditation, we gradually become more rooted and centered in the depths of our being through the faithful saying of the mantra.

John Main puts it this way:

> "More and more men and women in our society are beginning to understand that our personal problems and the problems we face as a society, are basically spiritual problems. What more and more of us understand in this world is that the human spirit cannot find fulfillment in mere material success or material prosperity. It isn't that material success or prosperity is bad in themselves but they are simply not adequate as a final or ultimate answer to the human situation.

As a result of the materialism in which we live, so many men and women are discovering that the spirit is stifled, and much of the frustration of our time is due to the feeling that we were created for something better than this, something more serious than just a day-to-day survival. To know ourselves, to understand ourselves, and to be able to start solving our problems, to get our problems and ourselves into perspective, we simply must make contact with our spirit.

Our spirit is rooted in God. Meditation is just this way of making contact with our own spirit, and in that contact finding the way of integration, of finding everything in our experience coming into harmony, everything in our experience judged and aligned on God.

Everything that we are, everything in our life, becomes aligned on God and everything falls into its proper place. Meditating is powerful because it leads us into this right order, into this tranquility, into this peace.

This is because our order of values has changed. Instead of our value system being based on the self, on the ego, on personal success or self-promotion, or whatever, on these limiting factors, our value system becomes based on God.

We discover, in the revelation that takes place in our own hearts, as we discover the presence of Jesus there, that GOD IS LOVE. This brings us to the conclusion that unleashes great power: that there is only one thing that matters ultimately, which is that we grow in love. Everything else is secondary. Everything is inconsequential. Once this insight becomes powerful enough, our lives are altered and we then see the greater reality of "other-centered" values such as compassion, understanding. We begin therefore to become truly spiritual people. We are then in touch with life at its center; and remember, God is the center, God is love, and Jesus is the revelation of his love."

LEARNING TO ABANDON DESIRE AND PRACTICE CONTENTMENT

One thing we learn in meditation is to abandon desire. We learn it because we know we are called to live wholly in the present moment. This sounds very strange to an achieving society, to people who have been brought up to practice so much anxious striving. The real tragedy of our time is that we are so filled with desire, for happiness, for success, for wealth, for power, whatever it might be, that we are always imagining ourselves as we might be. So rarely do we come to know ourselves as we are, and to accept our present position.

PRAYER AND THE SOCIAL DIMENSION OF THE GOSPEL

God's reign in our world is dependent upon the conversion of the human heart. Without this necessary conversion, the structural changes brought about by 'good works' eventually erode into evil systems that perpetuate different forms of injustice. Although conversion of the human heart and structural change must be worked for simultaneously, structural change remains the complement of the foundational change that burgeons systems of true peace and justice, namely, the conversion of the human heart. For our world to become a place where brothers and sisters are not deprived or ravaged economically, socially, and emotionally, the human heart must be turned from its propensity for egocentricity, which has produced the injustice and the lack of peace experienced in our world.

Contemplation is a path to this necessary conversion of the human heart. The works of peace and justice become the activity of those who know the experience of authentic prayer, because love of God and love of neighbor are inseparable truths.

Peter Ng

"To grow spiritually is to become less self-conscious and more simple. Progress in prayer cannot be measured except as we perceive a more pervasive spirit of love enter our daily life, as the Christian contemplative experience must bear fruit in the lives of others. The final word on how to pray is St Paul's first word on it – we do not even know how to pray, but the Spirit prays in us beyond all forms of language. Thus the guiding definition of Christian prayer is that we do not pray and that there are no methods of prayer. Our prayer is our entering the prayer of Jesus, his Spirit which is the stream of love flowing between him and the Father."

Laurence Freeman
Light Within, The Inner Path of Meditation

Sharing *the* GIFT

The Journey of
MEDITATION

THE LABYRINTH AT CHARTRES

As you enter the great 13th century Cathedral of Chartres through the west door you find yourself walking onto and into the Pilgrim's Labyrinth. The Labyrinth is drawn in black stone on the floor of the nave of the Cathedral under the Rose Window, whose diameter it reflects exactly. During the Middle Ages poor pilgrims, who were unable to go to Jerusalem, would make a symbolic 'pilgrimage' on their knees around all the twists and turns of the labyrinth in their own cathedral. In Chartres, as in many European Cathedrals where similar designs were once to be found, this spiritual mandala acquired great meaning in the devotion of the laity. Many generations experienced the joy of arriving at the center of the labyrinth after many doubts and hesitations.

If you trace the diagram of the labyrinth with your finger you will begin to understand why John Main considered meditation not merely a method of prayer but a pilgrimage and a way of life. Making the pilgrimage of the labyrinth with devotion, like meditation, illuminates the journey of our life. All the loops and backtracks of the labyrinth help put our times of acedia and apatheia, turbulence and peace, in the perspective of the overall design of the journey.

We begin at the beginning. Every human journey, even a spiritual one that transcends time and space, has a definite beginning. We are not far from the center even at the beginning, but we have a journey to make, a process of realization and self-discovery before we can find ourselves to be, in fact, already and always at the center. At the outset it seems we will get to the center on a straight run but we soon encounter the recurrent patterns of loops and bends that test and deepen our faith. They can make it seem we are losing ground, turning back; and after years of meditation we can think we have made no progress, except in the maturing of our faith, which is the essential meaning of spiritual growth. This same faith then shows us that the twists and turns of the journey are not a difficult God's way of making life more difficult, but a compassionate and wise teacher's way of untying the knots of our heart.

The labyrinth shows us the wisdom of not trying to measure our progress: precisely because the journey is not linear and mental but cyclical and spiritual, like the coils of a spring. All that matters is the confidence of knowing we are on the way. The path to the center is a narrow one but it leads to the source of life. Life is eternal at its source. We have only to stay on the path. If we try to cheat and jump over from where we are to where

we want to be without going the way we must go, we get lost and confused. But at any point we can start again. The ever-present compassion of God is experienced most directly in the constancy of the way and in the ultimate discovery, at the center, of the meaning of the journey we have made. We have only to keep moving forward in faith. Whoever seeks will find.

Meditation is a way. It is, first of all, a way of experience rather than of thought or imagination. Even a symbol such as the labyrinth points to this. A symbol such as the Pilgrim's Labyrinth of Chartres, though rich in meaning, is only truly understood when it is seen to point beyond itself and out of the world of signs altogether. Looking at an illustration of the labyrinth and tracing the journey to the center with your finger is very different from doing it in reality on your knees. How different then is the daily practice of meditation from merely reading or talking about it.

Excerpted from: "Christian Meditation Newsletter", March 1992

A PILGRIMAGE TO THE HEART

The journey of meditation, as John Main said (*Moment of Christ*) is essentially "a pilgrimage to our own heart", the most sacred place where the Holy Spirit, where Christ dwells. Meditation is "the life of the Spirit of Jesus within our human heart."

The fourth century Desert Father Evagrius, who was both a theologian and a practical man of prayer, describes with clarity the stages we go through on our spiritual journey. His writings show deep psychological insights into what is happening in us on this journey of pure prayer, unconceptual meditation. He was highly self-observant and self-analytical, and yet this was only in the service of his striving to become totally unselfconscious. To him the essence of life was prayer: "Go sell your possessions and give to the poor, and take up your cross so you can pray without distraction." Evagrius applied his mind to what the heart was going through, pondering what the experience of pure prayer was doing to him in terms of the overall healing process of life.

To him the journey started with the experience of conversion – 'metanoia', a change of mind, a new way of looking at ourselves and at reality.

When we first begin to meditate, we may feel the first fervor of conversion. The discipline seems easy and we start out with enthusiasm and commitment. Then follows an ever-deepening acceptance of the discipline.

The initial enthusiasm is tested and a deeper commitment is needed to the discipline, which is both outer and inner. It takes time to integrate the twice-daily meditation into daily life and it takes time to root the mantra in our heart. By repeating the mantra we gradually leave our self-conscious thoughts behind, "the chaotic din of a mind ravaged by so much exposure to trivia and distraction" (*Word into Silence*) and become aware of conditioned images of self and of God. But, in time, the discipline becomes a true necessity, a joy. We practice our meditation without demands for any results or expectations. Having a goal involves our own will and is the opposite of 'leaving self behind'. We become detached from both distractions and the joys of silence.

Then we enter a different level of thought – repressed memories, emotions and fears. This is at times painful and resistance occurs. "This is not surprising, for if a man came home to his house and found nothing but a smoking fire and a nagging wife, he would quickly run out again" (Walter Hilton quoted by John Main in *Word into Silence*). We are assailed by what Evagrius called the 'Demon of Acedia'.

Although he was modern in his perceptions, he was also a man of his time, and so unconscious psychological drives are seen as Angels or Demons, autonomous psychic entities.

Every meditator is familiar with the demon of acedia. He manifests himself as disenchantment with meditation and the spiritual path; we are bored and everything is tainted. We think we can find more useful things to do with our time than sitting down to meditate. We blame others and the environment for our own lack of attention. It is a time of dryness, boredom, restlessness, and distractions, with inner silence a thing of the past. God seems to be absent. There is no consolation and we are no longer aware of God's loving presence. St. John of the Cross called it the Dark night of the Soul. It is our 'desert experience'. It is a time of spiritual testing; we are tempted, as Jesus was tempted in the desert. We want to give up. Thomas Merton, talking about the desert experience, said, "Only when we are able to 'let go' of everything within us, all desire to see, to know, to taste and to experience the consolation of God, only then are we truly able to experience His presence".

All we can do is persevere in the faithful repetition of the mantra and accept its poverty. "Blessed are the poor in spirit, theirs is the Kingdom of Heaven" (Matthew 5:3). We accept our need of God and trust that God guides us, is present nevertheless, loves us and will never permit us to be tried beyond our strength.

This 'desert experience' is a purifying experience, a challenge to overcome our self-centeredness, to meditate without reward, without knowledge where we are being led, to meditate even when assailed by these deep distractions. Eventually we break through all resistance and are brought to self-knowledge, purified and strengthened. In this way the desert is also our way to the Promised Land. "No other demons follow close upon the heels of the demon of acedia, but only a state of deep peace and inexpressible joy arises out of this struggle".

This is apatheia, a deep imperturbable calm, the health of the soul. Now we have reached our essential identity. This is what we are, when the flow of thoughts and feelings has been stilled, when the ego-masks and false images of self have dropped away and the emotions are purified. This calm, this bliss, this peace and joy is at the same time perfect awareness, super wakefulness. It is being fully alive. "The Glory of God is a human being fully alive" (Bishop Irenaeus).

From there flows the final stage of agape, "the child of apatheia", the highest experience of all, a sense of oneness and of the universal, unconditional love of God. The knowable world of forms and all concepts of the mind are transcended. We know that "God is without quantity and without all outward form" and we "see with wonder the light of our own spirit, and to know that light as something beyond our spirit and yet the source of it". (WS). We know our spirit to be one with the Spirit. We have entered the stream of love between the Creator and the created. We have come home.

Although Evagrius presents the stages in a linear fashion, he was well aware that the journey is one of overlapping, deepening levels, spiraling with the stages reappearing, merging and transforming.

Spiritual progress cannot be measured in the same way as we measure physical well being or mental skills. St Paul's 'fruits of the spirit' are the true test of progress: a growth in love, compassion, other-centeredness and peace. "Happy is the monk who views the welfare and progress of all men with as much joy as if it were his own". Often others around us and near to us can perceive this gradual change better than we ourselves. It doesn't matter how long it takes, as long as we are on the Way. The stages of our progress will come about in their own time, God's own time.

> "Man must first be restored to himself that, making in himself as it were a stepping-stone, he may rise thence and be borne up to God".
> St. Augustine.

Kim Nataraja

STAGES ON THE JOURNEY

The journey of meditation offers deep insights into the life of the mind at its various levels and ultimately heals the soul.

A little diagram can help to show the levels of consciousness we all touch and pass through on the pilgrimage of meditation. Like all diagrams, and like the psycho-mystical systems of the great teachers of the tradition, it can also confuse if we think that it says everything or if we try to force our own experience to conform totally to it. Like a map it is meant to be used by anyone and so it is based on universal experience, but each one of us makes an unique journey and our own personal experience interprets the map even as we follow it. Meditation is a work, both our work of seeking God and God's work of seeking us. It is also a pilgrimage through the mysterious universe of the human person, an exploration into self-knowledge where the transcendence of egoism allows the unitive, non-dual knowledge of God to emerge. The meaning and the authenticity of our life depend upon this self-knowledge.

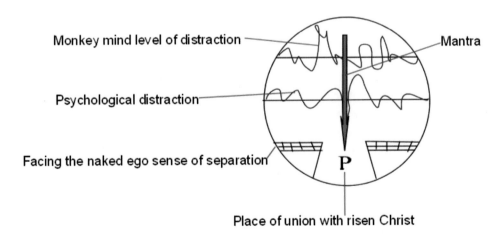

FIRST LEVEL

Anyone who has ever sat down to be still immediately engages the first level of consciousness a little below the immediate surface of the mind's daily functioning awareness. It is a rude awakening to the degree of indiscipline and restlessness in our monkey minds. St Theresa compared it to a ship whose crew has mutinied, tied up the captain and is chaotically taking turns to steer the ship. Some days may be better than others in terms of distractedness but even that only proves how wayward our surface mind is, how dependent on external conditions, how uncentered we are. So, we sit down, we start to say the mantra with faith and attention. Within three seconds (on a good day) we are drawing up a shopping list, or deciding what to wear in the evening or rehearsing the phone call we forgot to make earlier.

> "Therefore I bid you put away anxious thoughts about food and drink to keep you alive, and clothes to cover your body. Surely life is more than food and the body more than clothes." (Matthew 6:25)

> "We aim to be still in the present moment, which is the only moment of reality, of encounter with the God who is 'I Am'. Yet within seconds we are thinking thoughts of yesterday, making plans for tomorrow or weaving daydreams and wish fulfillment in the realm of fantasy. Set your mind on God's kingdom and his justice before everything else, and all the rest will come to you as well. So do not be anxious about tomorrow; tomorrow will look after itself."
>
> (Matthew 6:25)

Jesus' teaching on prayer is simple and pure, incisively wise and commonsensical. Yet it seems way beyond our capacity to practice it. Was he really speaking to ordinary humanity at all?

The discovery of our surface distractions is humbling. So, it helps to remember that it is a universal discovery, why else did Cassian recommend the mantra (he called it a 'formula') sixteen hundred years ago? Yet our own age has added to the problem of natural distraction by the enormous mass of information and stimulus that we must swim through every day, trying to absorb and classify it all from the moment we turn on the radio in the morning to when we turn off the television at night.

At this discovery it is easy to be discouraged and turn away from meditation. It is not my kind of spirituality. I am not the discipline kind of person. Why should my prayer time be another time for work? Often this discouragement veils a recurrent feeling of failure and inadequacy, the weak side of our damaged and self-rejecting ego, "I am no good at anything, even meditation".

What we need above all at this initial stage is an insight into the meaning of meditation and a thirst arising from a deeper level of consciousness from the one we seem stuck at. It is here right at the outset, therefore, that we encounter, although we may not yet recognize it as such, the prompting of grace. It comes from outside us in the form of teaching, tradition, spiritual friendship and inspiration. From within, it comes as the intuitive thirst for deeper experience. Christ, who as Spirit is no more within us than outside us seems to push from outside and pull from within.

It helps to understand clearly from the beginning what is the meaning and purpose of the mantra. It is not a magic wand that blanks the mind or a switch that turns on God, but a discipline, 'beginning in faith and ending in love', which brings us into the poverty of spirit. We do not say the mantra to fight off the distractions but to help us remove our attention from them. Simply discovering that we are, however poorly, free to place our attention elsewhere is the first great awakening. It is the beginning of the deepening of consciousness that allows us to leave the distractions on the surface, as waves on the surface of the ocean. Even at this earliest stage of the journey we are learning the profoundest truth, as we leave our religious as well as our ordinary thoughts behind: it is not our prayer but the prayer of Christ that concerns us. As the center of consciousness shifts from the ego to the true self, all notions of 'my' and 'mine' begin to weaken.

As long as we are living anything like a normal life this level of consciousness will be the first one we meet each time we meditate. On bad days and in dark nights it may seem we have never gone beyond it. But merely to be aware of it and to face it is to begin to transcend it. Gradually a change does take place at this surface level. We notice it first perhaps in the ways we are more able to sit quietly without needing to read a magazine or take an old anxiety off the shelf, impatience and a sense of the Presence of God in traffic jams or supermarket queues. A calmer and steadier mental life emerges in daily relationships. At meditation we become familiar, friends with, the patterns and habits of our mind and more tolerant of its wayward ways.

SECOND LEVEL

Reaching the second level, or zone, of consciousness does not mean we have forever mastered the discipline of the first level. We carry most of our faults with us all the way. At this next, deeper level we encounter the storage vaults of our lives. Everything we have done or said or thought or imagined, every impression, real or imagined, has its place here within the organic entity of our psyche. The great filing systems of this unique inner universe are our relationships, real and imagined, whatever has been done or said to us.

Here we must face what our unconscious processes have decided for us that we should not face. Lost, forgotten or buried memories with their attendant emotions and thoughts can be stirred up and released if they are blocking the movement of consciousness towards the true center of personal identity. Sometimes this work of healing, integration and self-acceptance can be as turbulent in its way as the surface distractions. Strong emotions, such as anxiety, fear or anger can emerge from nowhere and for no apparent reason. More rarely, vivid memories of forgotten events are replayed in the inward eye of the imagination.

Usually, however, it is work carried on below the surface of the conscious mind, out of the range of the ego's camera. The mantra then becomes like the seed in the parable of Jesus that a man planted in the earth while he went off and lived his daily life. All the time, the seed was growing in the dark womb of the earth, "how, he did not know".

If the danger at the first level is that we will become discouraged and turn back, there is another danger at this level. We may also find when the going gets tough at times that we demand some of the instant peace and consolation that we thought meditation promised us. But an equally grave danger is that we become fascinated with ourselves. The unconscious, as the light of consciousness penetrates it, has many strange and fascinating creatures to show us. There are many wonderful rooms to explore among the psyche's furnaces, workrooms, libraries and service centers. The faithful repetition of the mantra can seem rather uninteresting or distracting by contrast with these wonders. But fidelity at this stage has greater wonders to reveal that we can possibly imagine.

Self-knowledge, in the spiritual meaning of the term, is not restricted to what we discover about ourselves at this level of consciousness. But the full knowledge of the Self to which we are journeying is prepared for by what we pass through in this stage. It can be thought of both as purification and liberation and at times, when our deepest fears and shadows are uncovered, even as exorcism. From what happens at this level we become aware, at other times of reflection and prayer, of the major structures of our personality. We see the needs we had which life did not meet and the wounds that resulted. Wounds we hide or flaunt. Out of these wounds we can see the images of hope and happiness emerge which we then pursue down the highways and byways of life. We see the patterns in our relationships become visible and we can trace them back to ourselves rather than blame them only on others. We discover that we have become what we are because of how we have reacted and interacted (or refused to) rather than just from what was done to us.

Like all knowledge, this psychological self-awareness has equal potential for creativity or for destructiveness. It can spin a web of self-absorption and a shell of self-sufficiency. Or it can show us the power of forgiveness and tolerance from within the primary relationship with ourselves, and so empower us to live more fully and generously with all others in the bond of compassion.

Which direction this level of consciousness sends us in, is all-important for the rest of our journey. There is much solitude and at times true suffering at this level. Grace therefore gives us the love and balm necessary for our decision to persevere.

"He was among the wild beasts; and the angels waited on him" (Mark 1:13). Here above all we realize the relationship between meditation and community. As we become the person we are called to be we understand, that to be a person is more than being an ego, an individual in isolation. To be a person is to be in relationship. And so we discover something we cannot yet fully understand about the nature of reality itself: that God cannot be impersonal.

The turbulence of this level of consciousness is variable. At times there are great calms: stretches where we feel we are integrated and that we have got it together. Then our behavior one day or an inner swell of feeling from nowhere reminds us that this process will carry on for as long as we are making the journey. Similarly our surface distractions are there, perhaps unnoticed, even as we are absorbed in deeper thoughts. A fuller, more mature psychological self begins to form. We recognize it as bearing our name and appearance. We can own it without shame or regret and with love. Yet this very act of recognition and acceptance proves that this is not the end of the journey. This self we can look at and think about we must also leave behind. Earlier we left the busy, surface, daily self, running from one activity to the next. Yet with the opening of deeper levels we seem if anything busier than before. Life goes on at many levels simultaneously, all harmonizing with each other through the faith and love of the mantra. With this greater inner harmony we are ready for another deepening.

THIRD LEVEL

The ego has been our constant companion from the beginning. Now at the third level we meet it head on. At the first level we met it in its most frazzled state, dressed in the ever-changing costumes of daily life. At the second stage it is dressed in the more dramatic period costumes of the different stages of our psychological history, acting out its many roles as victim, exploiter, child, adolescent, adult, religious seeker, rebel or conformist; trickster, griever, lover, magician, warrior, king or queen.

It is from the ego that all resistance to this journey to the true self arises. And yet the ego is the vehicle of the journey as well. Typically today we focus on the vehicle rather than the journey. Just as we make an idol out of the motorcar, which is no more than an useful means of transportation, we can focus so strongly on the ego and its processes that we lose sight of the spiritual meaning of the whole person.

At this third level of consciousness, however, we confront the ego in its naked existence, all the costumes temporarily laid aside. *The Cloud of Unknowing* describes this stage as a 'stark awareness of your own existence' subsisting between God and ourselves. This awareness, too, the Cloud tells us, must go before 'we can experience contemplation in its perfection'. It is awareness touched by the deepest existential sorrow – not a sorrow about anything that has happened but at the fact of individual existence being inherently separate from Being. We must face and eventually transcend this existential sorrow before we can taste the joy of being.

Here too we understand the meaning of taking up our cross each day and following the Lord. Our cross is decorated by the trials of life but the wood of the cross is this naked sense of the separateness of the ego. No act of will can lift us over this final hurdle; no technique can whisk it away.

We are invited to sit at the foot of the cross at this stage in an ever-purer faith.

When waiting at a stoplight there is no alternative to patience. John Main remarked that more not less faith is needed as we pursue the pilgrimage. Here, where we face not merely distractions but the root and cause of distraction, our faith deepens and matures through the cooperation between our spirit and the Spirit of God until we are ready – the cooperation we see as synchronicity and call destiny.

The fidelity and maturity we have grown in during the earlier stages, stands us in good stead at this level. Our friend the mantra has by now become rooted and the earlier doubts and compromises present in the early stages of any relationship have given way. *The Cloud* reminds us of the need to be faithful to the 'one little word' 'in peace and war', just as Cassian insisted we say the 'formula' 'in prosperity and adversity'. John Main's emphasis on simple fidelity to the mantra 'from the beginning to the end of each meditation' is in this ancient tradition of Christian prayer, practical, helpful, wise. It makes full sense, however, only as our own experience teaches us.

WHAT HAPPENS NEXT?

A cartoon of two Zen meditators shows one asking this question of the other, who replies, 'What do you mean, what happens next, this is it!'

We have to be prepared for this being 'it' for a while. Yet faith is not just a matter of stubborn endurance. It is also a new way of vision. And as faith has grown so it enabled us to see something of what is beyond physical and mental perception. We know we are not waiting without hope or joy. 'You have not seen him, yet you love him; and trusting in him now without seeing him, you are transported with a joy too great for words, while you reap the harvest of your faith, that is, salvation for your souls' (1 Peter 1:8–9). Gradually and suddenly the light of a lamp shining in a murky place, as St Peter describes it, gives way to daybreak and the morning star rises to illuminate our hearts and minds (2 Peter 1:19).

The ego's naked sense of its own finite existence is like a brick wall we cannot get over by ourselves. In God's time and by free gift an opening appears in the wall of selfhood. In that opening of self-transcendence we leave self behind and find our true self in Christ. So at this moment an encounter occurs with the humanity of Jesus unlike any other meeting or recognition that occurred at earlier stages. Here we meet him in the pure non-dual action of the Spirit, beyond any image or idea we might have of him. This occurs in the reality of the Spirit that underpins all dogma and doctrine. (We put our faith in the reality to which the words point, as Aquinas said, not in the words themselves.)

As John Main said of this stage of the journey, we meet Jesus at the frontier of our own identity and he becomes our guide into the new country of God, the Kingdom. Everything Jesus said of himself makes sense through this encounter: door of the sheepfold, way, truth, life, resurrection, nourishing vine, friend.

Recognizing him in this encounter is redemptive. It concentrates our being in so fully personal and unique an experience of love that it becomes the standard of Truth by which all other experiences or insights must be judged. Here at this opening in ourselves and beyond ourselves we are illumined by the Spirit to make the journey with Jesus, in the mind of Christ, into the boundless love of God.

When will this happen? In a sense, because of the Incarnation and Resurrection it has already happened in each of us. It is only a reality waiting to be awakened to. Physics has discovered the dual nature of matter as being both a wave and a particle, depending on our way of looking at it. In the same way our pilgrimage of meditation through these different levels of consciousness can be seen as either successive, one stage following the other, or simultaneous, it is all now. Both are true, depending on the way we look at it. The way we see is decided by the depth of vision faith has clarified for us.

In that vision we can look forwards and backwards from the still point of the present moment. We can see how every stage of our journey, even the superficial levels of the distracted monkey mind, have been touched and guided all along by the Spirit who is now revealing Jesus to us, removing the veil. We now see how the deeper conflicts and wounds of our psyche at the second level are shot through with the healing power of the Spirit. And, as we see how every part of us lives and moves in God, the fruits of the Spirit begin to manifest themselves at all levels of our existence.

Laurence Freeman OSB
from "Web of Silence"

INTO THE PROMISED LAND

In this talk, I want to look at the psychological stages of the journey of meditation, what happens in our mind as we meditate twice daily over time. I begin by inviting you to reflect on the notion of 'journey' in general and to use as a guiding metaphor, our faith story of the journey of God's people from slavery in Egypt, through the wilderness, into the Promised Land. Let's take a moment to tell one another what we remember from that story. (See Exodus 12ff.)

Two things to note at the beginning are that the journey took forty years and that the Hebrews took a very roundabout route. It was definitely not linear but quite meandering. There are various reasons given for the length of the journey. Some say it took twenty years for one generation to forget about being slaves and another twenty years for the next generation to learn what it means to be free people. The Bible tells us that Moses knew the people were too weak to fight the various tribes they would encounter on the shorter route. Whatever the reason, the story reminds us that the journey to God/ Home/Promised Land is a process: a process of a growing sense of identity, of self knowledge, of knowing that they were God's people. Secondly, the story reminds us that the journey is a process of moving from chaos to order, it is a transition from a disorganized, motley group of Hebrews to becoming the twelve tribes of Israel. The journey home to God by way of the prayer of the heart, by meditation, requires time for us to let go of our slave-like ways, time to learn a new way of being, time to learn who we are.

It also helps us to remember that the roundabout route, the backtracking, the going in circles, the retracing of steps prepares us for the spiral nature of the meditation journey. There too, we keep discovering that we are going over the same ground as we learn to trust more deeply and to open ourselves to deeper healing and commitment. The Exodus story provides a helpful pattern to prepare us for a journey of depth as well as breadth as we meditate.

Keeping these two characteristics of the journey in mind, I want to travel with you through some of the common territory and stopping places that our mind encounters on the journey of meditation. Just like the Hebrews, we move in stages, camping in some places and then moving on. So pack your bag, travel lightly. You need only your longing for God, a quiet place, the mantra, and the will to pray twice daily. The itinerary unfolds as we journey.

Here we are. We have begun the journey, left Egypt and slavery behind, crossed the Red Sea. In silence and stillness, with only the poverty of the mantra, we begin. To our great shock we find we have traveled in our mind to Las Vegas! There is so much going on in our mind! – Lights that never go out, neon signs that beckon, casinos, shows, slot machines, dancers, entertainment, souvenirs, razzle dazzle. Such an attraction, such a distraction in our minds. We thought we wanted to begin this journey into silence. Why have we come to Las Vegas? We are like the Hebrews who longed for freedom and when they were on the path to freedom, went back to Egypt in their minds – longed for the food, the sights, the marketplaces of Egypt. We had no idea that our minds were so undisciplined. The silence of the wilderness seems only to show us how fragmented and distracted we are.

As teachers of meditation, what will we say to meditators who become frustrated that much of their meditation time is spent on scattered thoughts, minutiae, the shopping list, etc.? What will we say when beginning meditators are tempted to stop meditating because of the pervasive presence of Las Vegas noise? I think it helps to share that this experience is common to all meditators. It is the very reason we need the mantra. It also helps to acknowledge we live in a 'Las Vegas' culture with constant over stimulation of sight, sound and information. It surrounds us and it is not surprising that it is inside our psyche as well. But Laurence Freeman points out that if we can encourage new meditators to see their frustration at being so distracted 'as the promptings of grace', then they can get on with the journey. Like the Hebrews, we want our freedom but we first have to acknowledge all the ways we are enslaved, we have to become conscious of all that hinders our journey home to God. When we become aware that we long to be something other than the 'consumer' or 'slave' or however the culture defines us, it is this first stage in the meditation journey helping us realize what we don't want. In this first stage we begin to realize how much we long for a center, for unity, for healing.

I also believe this experience of our distractedness is very humbling and leads us to examine our understanding of prayer. We learn that the mantra is not a 'starter's pistol' that gets God going on our behalf – which is a way we sometimes think of prayer. Rather, we come to realize that prayer is opening ourselves to what God is already doing in us. The mantra clears a path so that we can listen to the Spirit of Christ speaking in our hearts.

As teachers, we can speak authentically of the 'Las Vegas' experience. We know that we travel there many times as we meditate. The Hebrews kept telling Moses their journey into the wilderness was a mistake. They had to learn how to live by faith. That is also true of the meditation journey. With faithful twice-daily practice, with encouragement from the group, knowledge that the journey is a spiral, we do move through this first stage. We learn to trust that the single word frees us from the distractions of the mind as surely as the Hebrews were released from the daily chore of making bricks. We learn to trust that the manna comes; the food for the journey is supplied by God's grace. We settle into the journey.

It seems that we have just settled into the meditation journey when we find ourselves in the Swamp. The water is black, covered with slime. Underneath all sorts of creatures are slithering beneath the surface, making strange noises. We have arrived in that area of the mind where we have relegated all those parts of ourselves that we do not want to own, along with all those experiences of wounding others and being wounded ourselves. We are confronted with our sins of omission and commission, our guilt, our fears, our brokenness, – all slithering around in the Swamp and we want to run. If this is where the meditation journey takes the mind, then it is time to stop! We were looking for peace and tranquility, looking to be more centered. This feels like the thirsty Hebrews being led to the waters at Marah only to find them too bitter to drink. It is like encountering the poisonous snakes. Yet, our faith story says that the water can become sweet, that which poisoned can become a sign of healing. Our faith story is inviting us to see the Swamp in our mind as a place of transformation and healing. As teachers we can encourage meditators by helping them to understand that their experience of the Swamp is part of the journey to self-knowledge. The awareness of our psychological wounds and our brokenness is an opportunity to bring to consciousness all that is in need of healing. Being in the Swamp is an invitation to look at the ways we have wounded others. It is an invitation to stop projecting onto others those parts of ourselves that we do not want to own and thereby opening ourselves to integration, to wholeness. In this second stage of the journey, we encourage meditators to keep on saying the mantra through this period, to seek the listening ear of a good friend or therapist. In time, we discover that the mantra is like the wood Moses threw into the waters of Marah – that which seemed too bitter to contemplate has been brought to consciousness and made sweet by exposure to God. That which was poisoning our life is changed into a symbol of healing. The great gift of the Swamp is that if we will keep meditating, we see ourselves being changed. As we accept ourselves in all our swampiness, we are more ready to accept others. As we experience the mercy and compassion of God, we are more ready to show mercy and compassion to others. As the motley group of Hebrews moved through the stages of their journey and found themselves becoming who they were called to be – God's people, a blessing to other nations, the people of Israel, so too do we discover who we are.

It is important to note that some people can get stuck in the Swamp, become so engrossed with the creatures in the murky waters that they are unable to move on. They are the ever-complaining Hebrews who cannot seem to move on. But hopefully, meditators do move forward through this stage. The nature of the journey is such that we do spiral back many times thorough the Swamp as well as through Las Vegas. But every sojourn in the Swamp helps us to realize we are unfinished, messy, and broken and in need of God's continuing grace and mercy. And so we journey on with a greater sense of self-acceptance, with greater kindness and love towards others. Our time in the Swamp has been life giving.

The third stage of the journey of the mind in meditation brings us to the Wailing Wall, the place where we confront our ego and discover what a golden calf we have built for ourselves. We discover that we have traveled all this way in search of God and a wall stronger than the walls of Jericho blocks the path. We cannot arrive home to God, to the Self, by blasts of the trumpet and by force of will. All the spiraling deeper and deeper has shown us that we are the barriers preventing us from arriving. We have been worshipping at the golden calf of human effort, of human desire. There is great grief at the Wailing Wall of the ego. Like those at the Wailing Wall in Jerusalem, we stick our petitions into the chinks in the wall trying to bridge the gap between the ego and the true Self. All our attempts only serve to show us how our ego is behind all our striving.

Our journey up to now has been about letting go – letting go of our monkey chatter which only keeps us in Las Vegas, letting go of our various slave-like ways and learning to trust in the poverty of the mantra. We have been learning to let go of our false self, our idols, our fears, our judgmental ways. We have been learning to trust in the mercy and love of God, to receive and incorporate it into our lives. In the process we are aware that God is shaping us, creating our true self and because of that awareness, a deep sense of joy pervades our life. To find ourselves at the Wailing Wall is a shock.

As teachers, I believe we can offer this very simple advice to meditators who find themselves at the Wall. Stay at the Wall and wait. No striving, no activity but rather enter into what I call Holy Saturday waiting. In the depth of our hearts we know that God has created us to be our true Self, that all is gift. We do not have to make it happen, we cannot make it happen. We stay at the Wall and wait and have occasional experiences that God has shone through a crack in the Wall. It is learning that I am truly myself when I align my will with God's will. Standing at the Wall is an invitation to simply 'be', to be in such communion with God that none of the ego is present. There is great liberation, great rejoicing.

In looking at the Exodus story as a guiding metaphor for the journey of the mind in meditation, I have been placing our personal experience of the journey into the larger context of our faith story. We see that the Exodus story is a reminder of God's love and faithfulness for God's people. Over and over, this story is the story of God's faithfulness on the journey. In the journey of the mind in meditation, we see the ways God continues to call us into freedom, into the experience that we are God's beloved son or daughter, into healing and wholeness, into becoming our true Self.

As teachers of Christian meditation, we have the great privilege of accompanying others on the journey. What I believe we do when we accompany others is simply 'profess' our own journey and by doing so we encourage and uphold one another on the Way.

Rev. Glenda Meakin

THE PSYCHOLOGICAL STAGES OF THE JOURNEY

> Meditation is a way of breaking through from a world of illusion into the pure light of reality.
>
> *John Main*

The world of illusion that John Main refers to in this statement is the world we build up out of our thoughts. Many of us equate who we are with what we think. Who do you think you are? The image we have of ourselves, the image we have of others, and the world we live in is made up out of thoughts: our own thoughts and, often, the thoughts of others we have unthinkingly made our own. From the moment we are born we accept the views of those who are significant in our life without question: our parents, our wider family, our community, our peer group, the society we live in, and the religion and culture we are brought up in. We shape our view of reality based on the accepted views of others in an attempt to fit in, to be accepted and respected. In other words driven by our need to survive, we adopt the opinions of others and adopt expected roles and attitudes. Often in doing so, we forget who we really are and become imprisoned by all this conditioning.

As we grow up, some of us have the self-confidence to challenge and examine these thoughts and views. We feel the urge to find out who we really are under all the conditioning, masks, roles, and functions. But 'breaking through' in the words of John Main, is not easy.

The fact that we are dominated by thoughts can be discovered the moment we start to meditate. We become aware of what John Main referred to as 'the chaotic din of a mind ravaged by so much exposure to trivia and distraction', whilst Laurence Freeman refers to 'the monkey mind level of distraction'.

'Breaking through', requires courage and perseverance, but will lead us to the 'pure light of reality', where we remember and experience that we are 'children of God', 'the temple of the Holy Spirit', and that 'the consciousness that was in Christ is also in us'.

The stages on the journey of meditation, our 'breaking through', are in fact our changing relationship with our thoughts.

SURFACE THOUGHTS

Meister Eckhart said in Sermon 12: "Three things hinder us from hearing the Eternal Word. The first is corporality, the second multiplicity, and the third temporality. If a person had passed beyond these three things, he would live in eternity, in the spirit, in oneness, and in the vast solitude; and there he would hear the eternal word."

By 'corporality' he meant being part of the material world, 'multiplicity' refers to images of self, and 'temporality' refers to images of God.

CORPORALITY

The first required change therefore is in our attitude to our thoughts about the world. These are the first layer of thoughts we meet in meditation.

We find it difficult letting go of our thoughts, since we have been brought up to believe that thought is the highest activity we can engage in. Descartes in the 17th Century said, "I think, therefore I am", and in doing so linked existence with thought. T.S Eliot illustrates this in his 'Four Quartets', in which people sitting in an underground train, stuck in a tunnel, feel they are faced with "the growing terror of nothing to think about". Not thinking feels like a threat to our survival. No wonder people are fearful when faced with a discipline like meditation that encourages letting go of thought. Will we still exist?

And indeed, the thoughts that race through our surface mind, in one-way or another, all stem from our instinct for survival. Most psychologists agree that we have a number of different needs in early childhood that need to be met to ensure survival: security, love, esteem, power, control, and pleasure. Initially, when we are young, we cannot meet these needs ourselves; we depend on others to do so.

Whether these needs are met or not shapes our emotional and psychological approach to life. If our upbringing was full of love and encouragement, we are likely to grow up self-confident, optimistic, and with a healthy self-esteem. We feel at one with the world and feel lovable. If our upbringing was loveless and critical, we tend to reject ourselves, have a low self-esteem, and suffer from insecurity, fear, and guilt. We feel unlovable and isolated.

Later we try to make up for this perceived lack by using material things and people to fulfill these unmet needs, still seeking their fulfillment outside ourselves, in the form of possessions, achievements, money, security, status and/or reputation. Even the roles or functions we adopt in society are partially a reflection of our unmet needs. They too give us a sense of security, identity, and belonging.

The world is not a hindrance; it is our attachment and attitude to it, our way of looking at and knowing reality. "If men thought of God as much as they think of the world, who would not attain liberation?" (Upanishads)

MULTIPLICITY

Linked with 'corporality' is 'multiplicity': the images we have of self. Both have their roots in our survival needs, as we have seen. We accepted the views and opinions of others: we see ourselves negatively as 'unlovable', 'powerless' 'incompetent' 'need to be in control', or positively as 'confident' 'lovable' 'intelligent'. We own these images; we are attached to them, especially to the negative ones. We are as much attached to our joy as to our pain.

Building our image of ourselves out of thoughts, needs, roles can result in the generation of many different, even conflicting selves. How often have you heard the phrase "I don't really know who I am anymore"? Our personalities are splintered and often we can feel alienated from ourselves. Eckhart called this being lost in "multiplicity" and in "alien images".

It is easy to see how these images are 'a thing that hinders'. How can we let go in meditation and trust, if we feel too insecure and need to be in control?

TEMPORALITY

The third 'thing that hinders' – images of God – is equally persistent. Our image of God is again inherited from early childhood, the cultural and religious beliefs we were brought up with, influenced by our attitudes towards parents, teachers, and society. Our images of God are often shallow and inadequate, and in many cases, distorted by our personal needs and emotions. We project on God human images and qualities. Just think for a minute on who and what God is to you personally? A stern, judging, and distant father? A being that only loves if your behavior meets certain conditions? How can you not feel guilty, when you have missed a meditation session, if you feel you have to earn God's favor and presence? Someone by whose attention you profit, if you abide by certain rules? Meister Eckhart illustrates the latter beautifully: "Some people, I swear, want to love God in the same way as they love a cow. They love it for its milk and cheese and the profit they will derive of it".

It is easy to see, how these views influence our attitude towards meditation. Moreover, we play the old emotional tapes, based on our flawed images of self: "You are out of control!, Are you not feeling powerless and insecure?", "You are unlovable! God can't unconditionally love you!" How can you "let go" in trust and faith, if you feel that love is conditional, is determined by how 'good' you are? And in our own view we are never good enough. We are our own worst critics! It plays on our individual weaknesses. However, you can press the stop button; you don't have to listen!

We may need images to focus our attention, but we must remember that they are "fingers pointing at the moon, but not the moon itself". They can never represent that which cannot be represented i.e. the unknowability of God. In the words of Meister Eckhart "I pray God to rid me of God". This is mirrored in the Buddhists saying, "If you meet the Buddha on the road kill him."

Often at this stage, we throw out the baby with the bathwater: the image is dead, so we think God is dead. It is important to remember that following a spiritual path means that our concepts of God will undergo continuous change. Spiritual maturity is the withdrawal of images and projections; however, we must be gentle when dealing with other people's images. The cry of Serapion, when convinced by others that he should let go of his anthropomorphic image of God at the beginning of Cassian's Tenth Conference, is anguished and heart rendering: "Woe is me, wretch that I am! They have taken my God from me, and I have no one to lay hold of, nor do I know whom I should adore or address."

If we do not become aware how emotional and social conditioning shapes our behavior and attitude, we remain automatons, reacting without thinking. We are then prisoners of the past and prisoners of our surface identity, our ego, our survival instinct, which clings to its separate nature, generating the illusion of separation from others, keeping you in conflict and competition with them.

Meditation leads us to a greater awareness of our conditioning and hence to self-knowledge and ultimately freedom.

One way helpful to entering the silence is to remember that all our thoughts are thoughts about the past or the future. And yet, only in the Now can we meet the Divine presence and its reflection in us. Only in the present Now alone does the world of time touch eternity. When Moses asked God who he should say sent him, the response was "I am has sent you" and Jesus stated when questioned by the Pharisees "Before Abraham was, I am." They therefore both emphasize that the Divine is pure Being. Meister Eckhart stresses "Amongst names none is more appropriate than 'He-who-is'" and states that the Divine Presence is only to be met in the present moment "standing in the present Now perfectly free in the will of God." That is the only "door". "Breaking through" can only happen when we are fully attentive to the present moment. Again Meister Eckhart "There is only one Now. Look!" The mantra is our way of staying in the present moment, fully focused and aware.

To let go of thoughts, to stay in the 'Now', however, is, as we all know from experience, easier said than done. I remember years ago there was an advert for meditation. On a poster there stood an Indian Guru, in typical attire and appearance, on his surfboard, balanced perfectly, riding the waves. Underneath was the phrase: "You can't stop the waves, but you can learn to surf". The mantra is our surfboard. You cannot suppress or get rid of your thoughts; they will be there just like the waves. You accept them as the part of you they are and just ride them skillfully. At times the thoughts and the waves calm down, the sea is smooth and calm, and thus your mind is still and at peace. We know then, that we are not merely the surfer, but the ocean itself.

DEEPER THOUGHTS

At this stage, when we enter the silence, it is important to remember, that the 'ego' does not want you to move out of its sphere of influence, it wants to keep you on the surface. It encourages you to identify with these surface thoughts, emotions, masks and roles. It does not want you to get in touch with the deeper parts of your consciousness, because it has deposited there any experiences that threatened your survival and it does not want you to deal with any of it.

We do need the ego, the survival instinct, but it is like an over protective parent, wanting to keep the child safe and close by, not allowing it to develop and learn independently. Going into the silence, is initially like leaving home, and then to arrive at your true home.

What does the ego do, when we take the plunge into silence? Often it increases our thoughts. When, however, we manage to surf those and enter the silence, the ego encourages us to let go off the mantra. We may convince ourselves, that the mantra disturbs the peace. If we listen to the voice of our ego and let go of our surfboard, we just float (or sink!) in "pax perniciosa" or "holy floating", and thus the ego has hindered our progress. If this fails, the ego may prompt us to ask "Isn't this boring, just repeating a word? What a con!" If we are still meditating, it might try a different approach, prompting us to ask, "Am I sure that this is the right method or the right mantra? Should I change my mantra?" Again the ego is making sure you are not going anywhere. If the ego fails to successfully hinder your progress, it might well try a final approach, prompting you to ask the question, "The teacher could be more inspiring and the group more supportive, should I look elsewhere?"

I am sure we have all met, at some time or other, these ploys of the ego to keep us on the surface.

It takes courage to leave 'self' behind, to leave the comfort of our conditioning. "Better the devil you know", we think. And yes, when we enter the forest of silence we meet both the beauty and the beast: both forgotten memories of beautiful moments and repressed fears. We are now in the psychological/emotional world, which John Main called: "darker level of consciousness of repressed fears and anxieties" and Laurence Freeman: "psychological distractions" and we see with the 'Eye of the Mind'.

Now we try to understand the world we live in and ourselves at a deeper level. Our thoughts and insights help us to reintegrate suppressed parts of our personality. We become aware of the roots of our behavior, and thus healing and integration takes place.

Slowly the 'things that hinder' fade.

Joy bubbles up, peace reigns, tears flow; feelings of anger and irritation come to the fore. Accept all that happens: the tears are the tears you did not shed, when you should have done so; the anger and the irritation were also not expressed at the appropriate time. Let these feelings come up, just accept them. Be aware of your feelings, without feeling the need to act them out. Letting these suppressed feelings come up is healing. They are frozen emotions, which are like blocks of ice, hold them up to the Light and Love of Christ and they will melt. There is nothing else to do but accept them and let them melt. There is no need to know the causes of these emotions: just name your demons and your heart will tolerate them better.

Sometimes hidden traumas surface and help is needed, but be aware that there lies the hidden danger of self-fascination or self-obsession. We could be in a cul-de-sac with nowhere to go, very much a prey to our thoughts and feelings.

The ego encourages us to "Let the past be! What is the point of reliving these emotions; they are better left alone!" Thoughts of "this is self-indulgent", that "we should do something useful for others" often appear. Many of us hold the philosophy that "an idle mind is a devil's playground". Conditioned thoughts concerning prayer may emerge i.e. "this is quietism!" as the ego resists our delving deeper by making it all seem pointless, dry, and boring. Don't fall for these tricks. You are free to choose to go into the silence of meditation. Trust and persevere. Remember that what happens is at a much deeper level that your rational consciousness. Meditation is beyond thoughts, feelings, and images. Your surface mind may be distracted, but at the same time healing takes places at the level your mind can't reach, at the level of silent communion with your deep consciousness and the consciousness of Christ. Persevere with the faithful repetition of the mantra, such that the mantra becomes the harmonic that sounds in your being and you are "lost in ... music heard so deeply, that it is not heard at all, but you are the music while the music lasts". (T.S.Eliot – Four Quartets)

SILENCE

With detachment from our conditioning, and detachment from the need to use the world and other people as emotional props, a different way of knowing emerges: we see with the 'Eye of the Heart': a higher, intuitive kind of knowing, direct and immediate. Then we enter the spiritual, transcendental realm, which John Main calls the "level of silence, where we see with wonder the light of our own spirit", "where we contact the ground of our being", and "where we experience the void", and Laurence Freeman "Peace, awareness of God's Presence", "facing the naked ego", and "sense of separation from God".

The more we enter the silence and stillness of meditation, the clearer our intuitive understanding becomes. We have left behind the 'things that hinder'. We see with Eckhart that "God is a light shining in itself, in silent stillness" and can feel, as described by Laurence Freeman, the "peace, awareness of God's Presence". At other times, however, we are very aware of a sense of "separation from God". Again, perseverance, faith, humility, and trust will melt the barrier we feel. It dissolves like blocks of ice in the stream of love between the Creator and the created.

Jesus refers to the "Eye of the Heart", when he says:

> "The light of the body is the eye: if therefore thine eye be single, thy whole body shall be full of light."

The whole purpose of meditation is to open this "single" eye by bringing the mind into the heart, so that our rational self no longer dominates our being. Our true self infuses the ego and the two are integrated. Then we are truly whole. Now we have become who we truly are.

It is important to remember that this is not something for the elite only; this is part of our human nature. One of the bedrock tenets of Jung's psychology is that there is an intrinsic drive towards wholeness and integration within the psyche of all people, which is also brought out by St Augustine:

> "The whole purpose of this life is to restore to health, the eye of the heart by which God may be seen."

Kim Nataraja

THE FOUR STAGES OF PRAYER AND MANTRIC MEDITATION
Teresa of Avila and John Main

"If you knew the gift of God and who is saying to you, 'Give me a drink,' you would have asked him and he would have given you living water ... Everyone who drinks this water will be thirsty again, but whoever drinks the water I shall give will never thirst, the water I shall give will become in him a spring of water welling up to eternal life." John 4:10

I. THE BUCKET

"The way we set out on this pilgrimage of other-centeredness is to recite a short phrase, a word that is commonly called today a mantra. The mantra is simply a means of turning our attention beyond ourselves – a way of unhooking us from our own thoughts."

II. THE WATER WHEEL

"Reciting the mantra brings us to stillness and to peace. We recite it for as long as we need to before we are caught up into the one prayer of Jesus."

III. THE SPRING

"The day will come when the mantra ceases to sound and we are lost in the eternal silence of God. The rule when this happens is not to try to possess this silence, to use it for one's own satisfaction."

IV. THE RAIN

"Gradually the silences become longer and we are simply absorbed in the mystery of God. The important thing is to have the courage and generosity to return to the mantra. I hope that it will become clear that each of us is summoned to the heights of Christian prayer ... to fullness of life."

John Main, Inner Christ, p.103;
Teresa of Avila, Life, Ch. 11–18

In John 7:38, Jesus says, "If anyone thirsts let him come to me. Let the person come and drink who believes in me. From her breast shall flow fountains of living water".

In Jeremiah, Yahweh says, "My people have abandoned me, the Fountain of Living Water, only to dig cisterns for themselves, leaky cisterns that hold no water". (Jer 2:13) And again, in Jeremiah, "The one who trusts in Yahweh is like a tree by the waterside that thrusts its roots to the Stream when the heat comes it feels no alarm, its foliage stays green, it has no worries in a year of drought, and never ceases to bear fruit". (Jer 17:7–9) And Jeremiah says in 31:9 to Northern Israel, "I will lead them back, I will guide them to streams of water ... their soul will be like a watered garden ..."

Isaiah 58:11 says "if you, my people, live a life of love and justice, Yahweh "will give strength to your bones and you shall be like a watered garden, like a spring of water whose waters never run dry".

So often is the metaphor of water with its properties of cleansing and fruitfulness employed in the scripture that it causes us today to again ask how it speaks of Grace and wholeness to us as we walk the spiritual path. What human and spiritual fullness is contained in this beautiful creature, water. Perhaps the Gospel turns our eyes to the way Jesus spoke about it. Come to me you who are thirsty. Or, to the Samaritan woman, "If you knew the gift of God and who asks for a drink of water, you might have asked and he would have given you living water" – "Whoever drinks this water will get thirsty again; but anyone who drinks the water that I shall give will never be thirsty again: the water that I shall give will turn into a spring inside him, welling up to eternal life". (John 4:10–15)

With this marvelous symbol of the Spirit – in Revelations' vision of "the river of life, rising from the throne of God and of the Lamb and flowing crystal-clear down the middle of the city street" let us look at how St. Teresa uses this image to guide us through the stages of prayer. Struggling to find an image to teach her mystical doctrine, which at the same time is emphatically her own experience, she draws on the beautiful story of the Samaritan woman's need, and relates that to her own experience and consequently to ours. Namely, this woman's search for meaning and acceptance illustrates our own thirst, our own emptiness and our own longing for wholeness. Notice how Jesus reveals her whole life and as we meditate, we too face the real self!

Water – Grace, the inflow of God's Love, the Spirit Who orders all things comes to our rescue in the and from the Person of Jesus. "Ask of me and I would have given you living water!"

John Main says that we begin on a pilgrimage of other-centeredness – turning our attention beyond ourselves and do so by reciting a short phrase, a mantra. How does this correspond with Teresa's First Water? Draw the water out of the well with a Bucket. This process, if any of us have tried watering our flowers with a bucket, will be tedious, sometimes muscle tearing, labor and time consuming. Teresa is talking exactly about that as we attempt to direct our intention to silence, prayer and doing it on a daily basis. All that she writes in all of her books are about prayer. In her own life, it took her 18 years after entrance in Carmel to surrender to wholehearted prayer. The fragmentation and mediocrity of her life left her longing but unrewarded in the inner peace she was seeking. In her second conversion as she approached her 40th year, new graces of intimacy and love began to flow. Her life changed. How can we hear Teresa's experience and derive help from it? We certainly will probably never experience the mystical events of her life. No matter! Her solidness as a guide does not derive from the extraordinary but rather from her teaching of compunction, discipline and those ordinary avenues of human effort which we are all capable of and which John Main also calls us to. Teresa's standard cry is "determination – a determined determination". This is the time for humility, poverty of spirit, and cautions us that "if there is no progress in humility – (truthfulness about our own inability to reach God on our own) – everything is going to be ruined". In fact, this is the time to come to a deeper self-understanding of our own incompleteness as the Samaritan woman. Here is what she says: "This path of self-knowledge must never be abandoned nor is there on this journey a soul so much a giant that it has no need to return often to the stage of an infant and a suckling!" Again, "Along this path of prayer, self knowledge and the thought of ones sins is the bread with which all palates must be fed no matter how delicate they may be; they cannot be sustained without this bread". (13:15)

John Main speaks similarly at this stage: "it is only in accepting silence that man (and woman) can come to know their own spirit". He goes on to say that we must confront "with some shame the chaotic din of a mind ravaged by so much exposure to trivia and distraction". True, he says, that our first inclination is always to retreat from the dawn of self-knowledge. If faithful, the fruit for Teresa and John Main is to know our absolute dependence on God. The first stage then is work – mostly our work of prayer, silence, waiting with attention, trusting the generosity of God who continues to call us and wait for us. Ego will object. Be prepared. "No time; fatigue; nothing is happening; wasting time etc."

The Second Water of Teresa's leads us deeper in to an unknown Presence who assures us of power, mercy and love. This is the stage of the Water Wheel – drawing water now with still some effort but also the new experience of being caught up in the one prayer of Jesus. John Main's beautiful phrase of "the stream of love flowing between the Father and the Son in the power of the Spirit" expresses our deepening contact, even if many times only momentary. We are now at that stage of reciting the mantra, aware of distractions but not bothered by them. For Teresa, change is taking place in what she terms as the "Prayer of Quiet" a graced experience of the gift of God's love and she says the beginning of all blessings There will be dryness testing us to continue the work without consolations at times and leaving the intellect go. What one must do, she says, is let the prayer proceed "gently and noiselessly. What I call noise is running about with the intellect looking for many words and reflections so as to give thanks for this gift ... The will calmly and wisely must understand that one does not deal well with God by force and that our efforts are like the careless use of large pieces of wood which smother this little spark ... One should pay no attention to the intellect, for it is a grinding mill ..." How clearly she cautions not to pursue the thoughts. Better to remain in the recollection like a wise bee. "For, she says, if no bee were to enter the beehive and each were employed in going after the other, no honey could be made!" (15:6) when one begins to compose speeches and search for ideas, let one know that there isn't any idea that will force God to give us more favor. So in this stage of the second water and the one prayer of Christ, the person is continuing faithfully with their one word, their mantra and experiencing the exhilarating, though momentary, Presence of the inner Christ. In this Presence there is no servile fear. Listen to Teresa: "He grants a more trusting fear. It is aware of the beginning of a love of God that has much less self-interest ... this prayer of quiet is the beginning of all blessings. The flowers are already at the point in which hardly anything is lacking for them to bud." (15:14–15)

The journey to stage three and the Third Water are represented by the Spring and John Main says the "day will come when the mantra ceases to sound and we are lost in the eternal silence of God". Again, the self-interest of the last water decreases and we are loving God for Himself not for our reward or gifts. It is the Giver now who occupies all our attention. The will has come into the Prayer of Union, a prayer Teresa will speak of in her *Interior Castle*. (dwelling place 5 on cocoon and butterfly). It will also bring a deeper awareness of the Cross. Part of that Cross is the knowledge of separation, which *The Cloud of Unknowing* talks about. There is detachment, wanting only to do the will of God and serve others. John Main is eloquent at this stage: it is now the dying of Christ that we carry and as he says, "we are led from depth to depth of purifying simplification until, having contacted the very ground of our being, we find the life we laid down and the self we surrendered in the Other". Again, he says "we are entering a void in which we are unmade. We cannot remain the person we were or thought we were. But we are, in fact, not being destroyed but awakened to the eternally fresh source of our being. We become aware that we are being created, that we are springing from the Creator's hand and returning to Him in love". Teresa echoes this: She says, "The water of grace rises up to the throat of this soul since such a soul can no longer move forward; nor does it know how; nor can it move backward ... This experience doesn't seem to me to be anything else than an almost complete death to all earthly things and an enjoyment of God".

John Main says that we must not try to possess this peace – this silence – since it is pure gift. This is the fruit of our twice-daily meditation. "Though our outward humanity is in decay, yet day by day we are inwardly renewed."

2 Cor 4:16 (the worm being transformed) But listen further to Merton as he addresses Teresa and John Main's Prayer of Quiet – "If there is one thing we must do it is this: we must realize to the very depths of our being that this is a pure gift of God which no desire, no effort and no heroism of ours can do anything to deserve or obtain. There is nothing we can do directly either to procure it or to preserve it or to increase it. ... At best we can dispose ourselves for the reception of this great gift by resting in the heart of our own poverty, keeping our soul as far as possible empty of desires for all the things that please and preoccupy our nature, no matter how pure or sublime they may be in themselves." (*New Seeds of Contemplation* p. 230)

For the fourth stage, Teresa's fourth water, the image of rain is the blessed gift of pure union – as far as possible in this life. John Main says, "gradually the silences become longer and we are simply absorbed in the mystery of God". Again, we must have the generosity and courage he says to return to the mantra, to accept in poverty and gratitude the immense favor God has given. Hear again Thomas Merton – "no effort, no heroism of ours can do anything to obtain it". And yet, John Main calls us to know that all are summoned to the heights of Christian prayer – the fullness of life.

As I was pondering this talk, it was raining gently and persistently for almost 12 hours. What grace to see the desert coming to life, the cacti and shrubs blooming in front of my eyes and reflect again the power of this image – God blessing us with union, the image of fruitfulness, the garden bursting with life. Teresa writes on this prayer: "In this fourth water the soul isn't in possession of its senses, but it rejoices without understanding what it is rejoicing in. It understands that it is enjoying a good in which are gathered together all goods, but this good is incomprehensible. All the senses are occupied in this joy in such a way that none is free to be taken up with any other exterior or interior thing." One moment is enough to repay all the trials that can be suffered in life! It is now that the Christian can say with Paul, "I no longer live, it is Christ who lives in me!" There are still no fewer trials and crosses – perhaps more. There is still the need to maintain detachment and now to understand it more fully. Again, Merton will say "We do not detach ourselves from things in order to attach ourselves to God, but rather we become detached from ourselves in order to see and use all things in and for God." There is still the need to maintain the daily twice periods of the practice of prayer and any slight self-trust is abhorrent. The fruits of this garden, saturated with the Grace of God's love, are readily available now for others and it is in their deep longing to share that the person spends their days. What also is apparent is the experience of integration. The active and contemplative are one; Martha and Mary walk together and experience great generosity and courage. The rain has fallen into the streams of the soul and the two have become one. "I no longer live ...". The perfection of this stage is in the communion experienced in the Spirit who is the Source, the Bucket, the Water-Wheel, the Spring, the Rain, the expansion of our being with the Being of God.

John Main says it best: "The communion we discover in the solitude of our own hearing and responding is not only communion with ourselves. That is perhaps the first sign we have of it – a deeper personal harmony and freedom. But it persists beyond, to the communion we share with all men and women, with all the dead and all the living and the yet unborn. (How beautiful that the end of that story of the Samaritan Woman is that she goes back to her village to spread the word!) With them we have the great and mysterious gift of life in the flesh and in the Spirit. And as we awaken to this deeper and higher sense of wholeness we sense the ultimate all-embracing communion, which contains all this, and of which these are epiphanies. The communion we have with God and the communion within God – this is the great truth we encountered. All we can say in the end is what we said at the beginning – that the meaning of life is the mystery of love." p.322 IC

When will this happen? Laurence Freeman says, "because of the Incarnation and Resurrection it has already happened in each of us. It is only a reality waiting to be awakened to".

Let me end with Isaiah:

"Oh, come to the water all you who are thirsty; though you have no money, come! Buy corn without money, and eat, and, at no cost, wine and milk. Why spend money on what is not bread, your wages on what fails to satisfy? Listen, listen to me, and you will have good things to eat and rich food to enjoy. Pay attention, come to me; listen, and your soul will live." Is 55:1

Joanne Rapp

Sharing the GIFT

Organizing a School of
MEDITATION event

INTRODUCING CHRISTIAN MEDITATION TO OTHERS

Now that you have reviewed "The Essential Teaching" and other background information, you are better prepared to share the teaching with others in evening, day-long, or weekend-long Christian Meditation events.

We now turn our attention to how to present the teaching. The following sections will help you to present the teaching to different types of audiences. You can never presume that your listeners have all had the same up bringing or that they share the same faith background. Since these suggested materials have been used by others before you, they should prove to be helpful to you. We encourage you, however, to personalize these materials as much as you can so that, you, in effect, make them your own, without distracting from the focus of the seminar. The Essential Teaching will remain constant while you use your own examples to illustrate the teaching.

As you know, The Essential Teaching is contained in the books *Word into Silence, Christian Meditation: Your Daily Practice* and *The Gethsemani Talks.*

Each Introductory Seminar that you give should include the following elements:

- The Christian Tradition and Context of Meditation
- The Simplicity of Meditation
- How to Meditate
- Meditation as a Spiritual Discipline and Way of Life
- The Community that Meditation Creates

You will be able to incorporate readings, audiotapes, and videotapes, along with your own talks during your teaching seminars.

PRACTICAL DETAILS FOR SETTING UP AND RUNNING AN EVENT

BEFORE THE EVENT

In deciding to hold an event it is important to consider:

- The Leadership: If you plan to lead the event, what support can you hope to call upon from other meditators. A good idea would be to plan the event with your group, or a few meditator friends. This will ensure adequate assistance.

- The Participants: Assuming this is an introductory event, who are the participants likely to be? You need to decide whether this is to be a local parish event, an ecumenical event, or a general event. Advertising is very important. It is good to place notices as widely as possible, but in accordance with your aims. For general events it is useful to place notices in secular places such as libraries, corner shops etc, and to advertise in the local press. Writing a brief article for your parish magazine, ecumenical newsletter, or local paper can be a good way of preparing for an event.

- The Venue: Choosing the venue is important. The audience you are seeking to attract can also influence this. The venue needs to be within your budget. Size, temperature, decor, and equipment are other factors to be gone into. If you plan to include the DVD *Pilgrimage*, then the availability of a DVD player is essential.

- Costing the Event: This can be a problem if you have no resources at your disposal. Sometimes a parish will help for a parish event or even a wider event. Or the local ecumenical group. If you are going to have to risk some financial outlay it is important to budget the event carefully to avoid loss. Costs before the event, may include the hire of the room, photocopying or printing, postage and travel. When setting a price for the event these items need to be taken into account. Two prices for events are useful, one ordinary and one for those on low income. In calculating the budget, the ordinary cost should be high enough to balance the price for those on low income. Such an undertaking cannot be entirely risk-free as you cannot ensure an adequate response. One way to overcome this, if it is essential to do so, is to work the budget on a minimum number and cancel the event if this number is not attained a few days in advance.

■ Flyers and Booking. The flyer (keep it simple!) for the event needs careful checking that all details are correct, and included. Date, time of start and finish, venue and how to get there. Cost and how to book with instructions on how to pay and who to contact for further details. If admissions will be accepted on the door this needs to be clearly stated. It may be necessary to send out further information to those who book. Information regarding travel, parking etc. Also it is important to have The World Community for Christian Meditation logo on the poster.

■ It is useful to have nametags for people, as this helps with introductions and getting to know each other. This applies mainly to longer events, it is usually not feasible for a short evening introductory session.

AT THE EVENT (BEFORE THE PEOPLE ARRIVE)

■ It is important to have arranged for sufficient help for this part of the event, so that when the people arrive there is time to greet them and welcome them etc. The atmosphere needs to be calm with a sense of readiness and warmth of welcome as people begin to arrive. This will set the tone for the whole event.

■ Arrange the room in such a way that it is welcoming, and has a point of focus. An icon, flowers and a candle can create this effect, especially if the room is bare as parish halls often are.

■ It is useful to have a display of books and tapes, flyers and other information about other events that you may have.

■ Good lists of those who have booked and amount paid or due as applicable will help with registration. Lists need to be in accordance with the way you have arranged bookings. Alphabetical lists help those doing the registration.

■ Any handouts or written information that you may have prepared can be given out with registration or placed on the chairs. (If it is a handout that supplements your presentation, you should distribute it during your talk, not as people arrive.)

■ Playing meditative music as the people arrive and take their seats will encourage an atmosphere of quiet waiting, unless of course refreshments are being served on arrival.

■ On weekend events it is helpful to allow registration to run between tea and supper, with tea available as people arrive.

■ If necessary it is helpful to place notices announcing the conference and pointing to the car park, entrance etc.

AS PEOPLE ARRIVE

■ This is a very important moment. People may be feeling shy or uncertain and the warmth and friendliness of the welcome does a great deal to dispose them favorably to what they are to receive.

■ The smooth running and clarity of registration and information allows an atmosphere of peace and quiet to be maintained.

■ When it is time to begin, it is helpful to be able to leave someone for a time at the registration point to welcome any late arrivals and show them quietly into the hall.

■ During the event it is good, whenever possible, to have more than one person who can be attentive to the needs of the participants. This person(s) needs to be identified to the group beforehand.

■ The longer the event, the more care needs to be taken in preparation and organizing the event as it happens. Teamwork and the community that meditation creates are essential elements to the seminar.

SUGGESTED SCHEDULES

AN EVENING EVENT:

7.00 – 7.30 pm   Arrivals & Registration (Coffee optional)

7.30 pm   Welcome & Introduction.

The method of introduction can vary depending on the size of the group and the time available. Introduce yourself, then invite those in attendance to say who they are and a little about why they have come. If you have broken a large group into smaller groups or into two's or three's, invite a few to share what they have learned about their group members. This is a way for you to get a feel for the group and what they are expecting and seeking.

7.45 pm   Introductory talk
Stretch break, if not at the beginning.
20–25 minute Period of Meditation
Coffee break
Question and answer period.

About 9.15 pm   Concluding information.
Signing up for those who want to receive the Newsletter.
How to contact groups: have the contact number for the local group available on hand-out sheets.
Ordering books and tapes, etc.

Always be available for those who may want to ask a question or make a comment privately before they depart.

AFTERNOON (HALF-DAY):
(Times vary according to circumstances)

2.00 pm	Arrivals & Registration
2.30 pm	Welcome and Introductions as above. (Brief silence for gathering is helpful to include somewhere in the introduction time.
2.45 pm	Introductory talk (about 30–45 min.) Stretch break 25 min. Period of Meditation Questions and answer period
4.30 pm	Tea/coffee
4.45pm	Video *Pilgrimage* or second talk. (See suggestion section for second talks)
5.15 pm	Summing up as above.

DAY EVENT:
(Times vary according to circumstances)

10.00 am	Arrivals & Registration (Coffee and Tea are optional)
10.30 am	Welcome and Introductions as above.
11.00 am	Introductory talk Stretch Break 25 min. Meditation
12.30–1.30 pm	Lunch Break
1.30 pm	Question and answer session
2.00 pm	*Pilgrimage* video or Second talk. Followed by sharing and questions. Alternatively, some practice and exercises in stretching, relaxing and breathing could be included. Tea/coffee
3.30 pm	25 min. Meditation
4.00 pm	Concluding remarks as above. Departures.

If the day is longer, a period of silent reflection could be put in, possibly on a chosen text. This could also be done in groups, with or without feedback. Suggested essential elements two meditations and two periods of information. Some simple stretching exercises and learning more about posture and breath could also be included if the leader or someone else has the skill for this.

WEEKEND EVENT:

Any of the rcorded retreats of Laurence Freeman could be used as added input or recordings of John Main. However, the leader needs to give some personal input according to recommendations in this handbook. For a weekend it can be helpful and useful to have a theme as well as the introduction to meditation. E.g. "Meditation and Wholeness", "Aspects of Love", "Meditation and the Spiritual Journey", "Living in the Present Moment", etc.

Friday evening

- Welcome and Introductions, here it is advisable to allow each person to introduce him/herself and share hopes, expectations etc. This gives the leader a feeling for the needs and situation of the group.
- Short introduction to the weekend and the schedule.
- Short period of silence (about 5–10 min.)
- Night Prayer. Compline is very useful if available.

Saturday

Before breakfast   Morning Prayer and Meditation with brief instruction on how to meditate.

Morning   Introductory talk.
Coffee Break
25 min. Meditation session
(This can be preceded by instruction, stretching, breathing and how to sit.)
Questions and or shared reflection on the experience.

Lunch
Free time (with suggested theme for reflection)

Tea/coffee
Second talk (see suggestions) or
Recorded talk of John Main or Laurence Freeman.
Sharing and discussion together or in groups.

Before supper   Meditation and evening Prayer.

Supper
Another short talk or recording or *Pilgrimage* video.
Night prayer & optional meditation

Sunday

Before breakfast   Meditation and Morning Prayer.

Breakfast

(Depending on the place, the composition of the group, and the availability of a priest, a Eucharist or ecumenical service or agape of some type can be built into the day).

> Another talk on the theme of the weekend which expands on the introduction and introduces new material.
> Coffee break
> Period of meditation (with stretches, breathing etc as required)
> Followed by more time for questions.
> Or if there are experienced meditators present, two or three people could witness to role of meditation in their lives.

Lunch

Concluding Session
The closure of any event is very important. The following points need to be considered.

Evaluation: It can be very valuable to have a simple evaluation form to hand to participants at the last session. This is a way of assessing how the event has been perceived. It can also give you ideas and guidelines for future events. The longer the event the more useful it is to have an evaluation. Probably it is not advisable for an evening introduction as time is too limited.

Looking ahead: It is very important to ensure that people are given adequate information about how to keep in contact, receive the newsletter, find their nearest group etc. This needs to be spoken of clearly and, preferably, lists left out for people to sign. If there is no group in the area as yet and it is clear that there is a need, it is important to spend time discussing and seeking ways for a group to begin. It is useful to note likely people during the session and approach them one to one to speak with them about the possibility of starting a group. Be clear about what support is available for anyone starting a group. This should be offered and made readily available to anyone interested. (See appendix for resources.)

Support for the Journey: Depending on how community and the tradition and teaching have been dealt with during the event, it is important to stress the difficulty of carrying on alone. The main reason for the existence of the WCCM is as a community which provides support to meditators in various ways. The fact of community rather than organization needs always to be stressed. This will bring in the importance of groups, but also the value of the resources available to groups and individuals. The teaching value of the newsletter, books and recordings needs also to be emphasized. Contacts with the National Centre and network including the calendar of events, where these exist, is another means. Help may also be found through the Community Web pages at http://www.wccm.org

Sharing *the* **GIFT**

INTRODUCTORY
Talks

INTRODUCING MEDITATION TO A MAINLY CHRISTIAN AUDIENCE

Depending on your audience and the length of time available select relevant points.

- Introduce yourself and situate yourself to the group briefly within The World Community for Christian Meditation. Describe briefly how you came to meditate. Then lead the group into silence for a few moments, before opening with a suitable scripture passage and comment on it in a way that establishes meditation as a way of prayer, deeply rooted in the Christian tradition.

- Choose one or two passages according to your inclination and your audience.
  For example:

Matthew 6:6	interiority, few words
Matthew 6:8	trust
Matthew 6:25	abandonment of worries, mindfulness
Ephesians 3:14–21	interiority, love fullness of being
John 14:19–20	mutual indwelling, Christ-centeredness,
John 15:4, 5–6	unity, interiority
John 17:21	

  (For other suggested passages see Gregory Ryan, *The Burning Heart*)

- Or use other supporting quotations from the Saints or authors relevant to your particular audience.
  For example:

St Augustine:	"If you know it, it isn't God."
St Augustine:	"The whole purpose of life is to restore to health the eye of the heart, through which we see God."
Hildegard Von Bingen:	"Prayer is nothing but inhaling and exhaling the spirit of the Universe."
Father Bede Griffiths:	"Prayer is the practice of the presence of God."
Meister Eckhart:	"All the images we have for God come from our understanding of ourselves."
Meister Eckhart:	"I pray God to rid me of god."
Wittgenstein:	"Concerning that which cannot be talked about, we should not say anything."

(For other useful quotes see Paul Harris, *The Fire of Silence and Stillness*)

■ Draw attention to the fact that in many denominations, there is an over-emphasis on doing – parish activities, committees, etc. Bring out the distinction between being and doing. We all may be 'doing' too much. Look at the story of "Martha and Mary" (Luke 10:38–42). Suggest that the quality of our activity depends on our 'being', being at peace with ourselves and being interiorly silent so as to be able to listen to others.

■ Highlight the universal phenomenon of the hunger for deeper spiritual life, why are people leaving the Church. Reflect on reasons, especially for the young.

■ Stress the universal tradition of meditation, not just an eastern tradition, but also rooted in our Christian tradition and bring out the basic theology of prayer (as much as time allows). St Augustine said that Christ teaches us because he prays in us and for us.

Matthew 5:3	poverty of spirit
Matthew 6:6	interiority
Luke 9:23	leaving self behind i.e. self-consciousness
Luke 10:21	revelation to the 'simple'
Mark 10:15	childlike, humble, loving trust
Romans 8:26–27	true teacher within
1 Cor 3:16	indwelling spirit
Acts 17:28	Christ-centeredness
Gal 2:20	Christ-centeredness
John 4:24–25	God is Spirit
John 10:1–11	Fullness of Life
John 17:21	Unity

John Cassian and the Desert Fathers: the tradition of 'pure prayer'
Hesychast tradition of the Jesus Prayer: (cf. Luke 18:13–14) "Lord Jesus Christ, Son of God, Have mercy on me, a sinner."
Cloud of Unknowing: "a little word," 'God' or 'Love'.
John Main and Laurence Freeman: "Maranatha"
(Background: Useful resource – audio by Laurence Freeman: "All and Nothing")

■ Introduce John Main and his rediscovery of the Christian tradition of meditation in John Cassian. Highlight the fact that John Cassian is a teacher acceptable to all Christians and lived long before the splits in Christianity occurred. Bring up scandal of Christian division, referring to either Luke 22:24–27 or Mark 10:42–46 or Matthew 20:25–26 and point out the ecumenical interest in meditation. It is a natural way for Christians to pray together, while words and ritual can divide us. Deep prayer shows us we are already "one in Christ". "For where two or three are gathered together in my name, there am I in the midst of them" (Matthew 18:20). Meditation does not eradicate differences, but we view them in a more gentle and forgiving way. Differences need not be divisions. Bring out meditation as the way to a theological balance, as it is not discursive and not dogmatic, but experiential. It acts as an antidote to fundamentalism by respecting differences and learning to forgive one another from the *heart*. Both diversity and unity (Mark 9:38–41). Jesus showing tolerance and respecting differences. Meditation is coming home to oneself, to one's personal relationship with Christ and to our original Christian unity.

Background reading:

John Main: *The Gethsemani Talks*

Paul Harris: *John Main by Those Who Knew Him*

Laurence Freeman: *The Life & Teaching of John Main (Audio)*

- ■ Present meditation as the missing link in our chain of prayer. It completes and enhances, not replaces other forms of prayer. It enriches scriptural prayer especially. Stress that meditation is a dimension of prayer that leads to silence. We are not speaking to God, not thinking about God, but *being with* God, being in communion with the presence of Christ within our hearts. Silence is "worship in spirit and truth."

  Use the image of the 'Wheel of Prayer' from the video *Coming Home* found earlier in this Handbook.

- ■ Highlight John Main's importance as a spiritual teacher. He has contributed greatly to the recovery of this spiritual tradition and the contemplative dimension and he stressed that meditation was for everyone. Emphasize aspects of his story to suit your audience. "Meditation is as natural to the spirit, as breathing is to the body" John Main. After the death of John Main, Laurence Freeman has led The World Community for Christian Meditation.

- ■ Emphasize the simplicity of meditation, not a complicated technique, no difficult theories to master, but it does require discipline – twice-daily practice leads to continuous prayer.

- ■ Introduce the concept of a *mantra*, a Sanskrit word, but now in the Oxford English Dictionary and used in daily life, meaning "that which clears the mind". (John Cassian's term "formula" was translated by John Main as "mantra"). We are using it in the sense that the "Way of the Pilgrim" speaks about the Jesus prayer, something we repeat in the heart. John Main recommended "Maranatha" – an important prayer in Aramaic for early Christians. St Paul uses it in 1 Cor 16; St John ends Revelations with it and according to modern scholars it was a password for early Christians to enter Eucharistic celebrations. It means: "Come Lord" and "The Lord comes".

- ■ Explain the purpose of the mantra. It simplifies and unifies the mind by freeing it from distractions. The result is alert stillness, focused on God. By silencing our thoughts, we "leave self behind" (Luke 9:23) and become more attentive to God and so to others. By limiting ourselves to the "poverty of the single verse" we become "poor in spirit" (Matthew 5:3). "Set your minds on the Kingdom of God and his justice before everything else" (Matthew 6:33–34). Explain how to say the Mantra: gently; don't evaluate; don't expect to achieve anything; don't use it as a club to beat your thoughts with; say it with faith and love.

■ "Unless the mantra is accompanied by faith and love, it has no real value; it would be merely a mechanism. It is a real danger to trust the mechanism of the mantra. But as an expression of faith and love, it becomes a very powerful means to direct your faith and to open you to God." (Bede Griffiths)

■ See Section on The Way of the Mantra and metaphors for the Mantra.

■ Bring out the fruits of meditation. By silencing our everyday thoughts and by focusing our attention on God, we are opening ourselves to the work of the love of God in our being – and so "Maranatha" becomes a powerful call of love. The effect is therefore totally life-changing, opening up the contemplative dimension of living. Fruits of the Spirit (Gal 5:22) best describe the changes. We are not trying to make anything happen during the meditation itself, but to realize what the Lord has already achieved in us.

■ See Section on the Fruits of the Spirit.

■ Stress that we should not evaluate our meditation. Failure and success are not relevant terms to describe the experience of meditation. They are ego-terms. Wondering about spiritual progress is really part of self-centeredness. John Main says that meditation is about taking the searchlight off ourselves, it is about losing our self-consciousness. We are learning "to leave self (the ego) behind." The only real test of spiritual growth is an increase in simplicity, love and compassion for others in daily life.

■ Stress the value of an ongoing group. The importance of meditation as a builder of community. We are on a journey together that creates community and connectedness, love of God, love of neighbor, love of self as one reality.

■ Use stories that emphasize how the Christian life and faith is being enhanced by meditation and how it helps the marriage of action and contemplation. Moreover, how it creates a more sincere and authentic Christian for the next millennium. Tell of your own experience of coming to meditation and your commitment to it.

Resource: Paul Harris: *Christian Meditation by Those Who Practice It*

■ Prepare group for meditation (see *Your Daily Practice*). Choose suitable music or chant with a group used to liturgical singing.

■ Meditate for 25 – 30 minutes.

■ Discussion. Invite questions and comments. Encourage practical questions, however 'basic' they may seem to the person asking. Emphasize simplicity and the way we learn from our experience. Offer your own experience of learning the discipline. Invite people just to begin. Refer to the books of John Main. Inform people about the weekly group, newsletter and other resources for getting started with a personal daily practice.

Adapted and summarized from discussions at the
first School for Teachers – Florence 1997

INTRODUCING MEDITATION TO A MIXED OR LARGELY SECULAR-MINDED GROUP

Depending on your audience and the time available select relevant points.

- Introduce yourself and situate yourself briefly within The World Community for Christian Meditation. Describe briefly how you came to meditate and then lead the group into silence for a few moments. Bring out that meditation is a spiritual tradition found at the heart of every religion, including Christianity.

- Explain meaning of the word "meditation". The Latin "meditatio" finds its origin in "stare in medio" meaning "to remain in the centre". The Latin word "Meditare" was used to translate the Greek word "meletan" meaning "to repeat". The prefix "med-" suggests (as in medicine) care, attention and concern. All these meanings reflect what meditation is: to be attentive with our whole being to a word or phrase we repeat. Its resulting centeredness stills the body and the mind, so that the spirit can grow. To grow spiritually is to become less self-conscious and more open to Love. "Contemplation", which is often used as a synonym, comes from the Latin "contemplare", meaning "to be in the temple with", that is, "in the presence of God". Father Bede Griffiths said, "Prayer is the practice of the presence of God" and 1 John 4:9: "God is Love".

- Refer to meditation techniques used for relaxation and health, which may be effective in their own way, but that here the emphasis is on a spiritual discipline. Meditation is not a theory, but a way of experience involving body, mind and spirit, leading to silence, stillness, and simplicity. Underline importance of meditation as a discipline, a daily practice.

- Highlight the universal hunger for spirituality today, the search for a deeper experience, especially amongst young people. Discuss meditation as a way of wisdom, including the aspect of self-knowledge.

- Meditation is the way of "coming home" to oneself first, then to God. Meister Eckhart said, "God is at home, it's we who have gone for a walk". "Being attentive", "being at home" helps one to deal with the contemporary problems of society with its stress and lack of moral consensus. John Main said:

"More and more men and women in our society are beginning to understand that our personal problems and the problems we face as a society, are basically spiritual problems. What more and more of us are understanding in this world is that the human spirit cannot find fulfillment in mere material success or prosperity. It isn't that material success or prosperity are bad in themselves but they are simply not adequate as a final or ultimate answer to the human situation.

As a result of the materialism in which we live, so many men and women are discovering that their spirit is stifled, and much of the frustration in our time is due to the feeling that we were created for something better than this, something more serious than just day-to-day survival.

To know ourselves, to understand ourselves, and to be able to start solving our problems, to get our problems and ourselves into perspective, we simply must make contact with our spirit.

As we live in both a material and spiritual reality, a Christian believes that he can experience the centre of all reality in Jesus Christ, who was spirit made matter.

Contrast complexity of modern life with the simplicity of meditation, the quiet repetition of the Mantra, in simple faith twice daily, day after day. No quick-fix, but steady simple discipline."

■ Introduce John Main and his rediscovery of the tradition of meditation in the Christian tradition of John Cassian and the Desert Fathers in the 4th Century.

■ Busy? Meditation creates energy, creates peace, and so reduces stress and anxiety, therefore better able to cope.

■ Use relevant stories about meditators. Resource: Paul Harris: *Christian Meditation by Those Who Practice It*.

■ Speak about the fruits of meditation in daily life (Fruits of the Spirit in St Paul – Gal 5:22), especially in human relationships with self and others helps you to get into a right relationship with yourself, and then naturally with others, the environment, society and the mystery beyond words we call God. 'Love yourself as your neighbor'. Once relationships get clearer, life draws on deeper inner resources. They are the key to personal and professional happiness. Meister Eckhart said, "Relation is the essence of everything that exists". Meditation clarifies, simplifies and unifies the mind by freeing it from distraction and this 'clarity' leads to 'charity'. By silencing our thoughts, we 'leave self behind' (Luke 9:23). See Section on 'Fruits of the Spirit'.

- Talk about the Rule of St Benedict as an ancient western description of harmony of life that is highly productive, well organized and spiritual. It reconciles body, mind and spirit, and the individual and the community by regular times of prayer. His motto was "Work and Pray".

- Point out that meditation is the spirituality of a global community, it is a natural bridge between religions, respecting religious differences but overcoming divisions, fear and prejudice. By leaving thoughts, words and images behind, we tread the common ground of the mystery underlying all reality. Talk about the Christian/Buddhist dialogue between our Community and the Dalai Lama, the John Main Conference "The Good Heart" and the "Way of Peace" Program.

- Meditation is about discovering fullness of life and becoming fully alive. "I have come that men may have life, and may have it in all its fullness" (John 10:10). John Main said, "The purpose of meditating is to advance along the way of the fullness of your own humanity. Meditating is simply accepting the gift of your own creation, and developing the potential to respond to the gift fully. We are not people who have to live on the surface, or people who are condemned to live lives of shallow emotions. Meditating is leaving the shallows, leaving the surface, and entering into the depths of your own being. In the Christian tradition, meditating is simply being open to the Spirit of Love, the Spirit of God."

  Going through death (change, disappointment, loss) to fuller life (joy in simple things, peace in times of difficulty). Reaching a state of balance and harmony.

- Mention the sacredness of the body, being present, even in illness or pain. Being in the present moment. The best way to take care of the future is to take care of the present moment. Meditation is not a 'mental' experience only, but integrates body, mind and spirit.

- Stress the value of an ongoing group. It encourages people to persevere in meditation and support them in periods of dryness. Meditation is important as a builder of a sense of community. We are on a journey together and that creates community and connectedness. Love of God, love of neighbor, love of self as one reality.

- You might compare this with AA.

- Lead group in the practice of meditation. (Resource: *Your Daily Practice*)

- Meditate for 25 – 30 minutes.

■ Discussion. Invite questions and comments. Encourage practical questions, however basic. Emphasize simplicity and the way we learn from our experience. Offer your own experience of learning the discipline. Invite people just to begin. Refer to the books of John Main. Inform people about the weekly group, newsletter and other resources for getting started with a personal daily practice. Mention the Web pages.

Adapted and summarized from discussions at the
first School for Teachers Florence 1997

Sharing the GIFT

SAMPLE
Talks

SUMMARY OF THE TEACHING

earning to meditate and learning what meditation has to teach us are both different kinds of learning from what we are used to. We are not learning anything 'new' in our usual understanding of novelty. We are relearning something known in childhood and lost before we could maturely integrate it. We are unlearning much, conditioned by our education and training, that is inadequate for a fully developed life. What we are learning by this process of relearning and unlearning is something too direct and simple for us to understand, except in and through experience. We are too complex and self-conscious for the experience when we begin. Some teaching, not only by example (the best teaching) but also by words and ideas, is needed to keep us on the way that prepares us for the 'magisterial experience' itself. Let me try to summarize this most simple of teachings, the essential elements of meditation. Let me begin by placing us in the context of the essential Christian teaching in the Scripture. St Paul here is reflecting upon the potential we all have for a richer and fuller life, for a life rooted in the mystery of God.

> "I kneel in prayer to the Father, from whom every family in heaven and on earth takes its name, that out of the treasures of his glory he may grant you strength and power through his Spirit in your inner being, that through faith Christ may dwell in your hearts in love. With deep roots and firm foundations, may you be strong to grasp, with all God's people, what is the breadth and length and height and depth of the love of Christ, and to know it, though it is beyond knowledge. So may you attain to fullness of being, the fullness of God himself." (Eph. 3:14–19)

This is a marvelously comprehensive description of the destiny that each of us has, as Christians, as human beings. Our destiny and call is to come to a fullness of being which is the fullness of God himself. In other words, each of us is summoned to an unlimited, infinite development through the way of faith and love, as we leave the narrowness of our ego behind, and enter into the ever-expanding mystery of God's own self.

The one quality we need to begin is courage. Beginning to meditate is like drilling for oil in the desert. The surface is so dry and dusty, that you have to take on faith the findings of the geologists who tell you that, deep within this dry earth, there is a great source of power. When we begin to meditate for the first time we cannot help expecting something to happen, that we will now see some vision, now come to some deeper knowledge. But nothing happens. Persevering past this stage, one of many hurdles our faith will encounter leads us to see that quietly at work in the heart of faith is love. When we see this, that it is not only by faith that we proceed but by faith and love, then we have really begun. Through this faith Christ dwells within us in love. His indwelling is the constant companionship of the teacher. Our initiatory courage has led us to find a teacher.

But it really is because 'nothing happens' that you can be sure that you are on the right path, the path of simplicity, of poverty, of an empowering surrender. Jesus has told us that his Spirit is to be found in our hearts. Meditating is uncovering this truth as a present reality deep within ourselves at the center of our lives. The Spirit that we are invited to discover in our hearts is the power source that enriches every aspect and every part of our life. The Spirit is the eternal Spirit of life and the eternal Spirit of love. The call of Christians is not to be half-alive, which means being half-dead, but to be fully alive, alive with the dynamos of the Spirit, with the power and energy that St Paul speaks of, and that is continually flowing in our hearts. To liberate this power is to be liberated ourselves. Liberty follows, if we will undertake the discipline to make our way to it, day by day. The way of meditation is simplicity itself. We only have to begin simply and to continue simply. It is essential to tread the path, to be on the way, each day of our lives. Because the Spirit is continually flowing in us, carrying us with it towards God, we must be continually uncovering it.

A very effective sign of this continuity of presence is the physical stillness we discipline ourselves to adopt during meditation. It is something we need to learn, to relearn as we unlearn our conditioned restlessness. We simply place our body on the cushion, in the chair, and we leave it there, totally devoted to the work of meditation. This is the first step away from egoism and from our compulsive concern with ourselves as we open our consciousness to what is beyond ourselves, the limitless reality that expands our spirit into an unpredictably generous, selfless love. The challenge that each of us has to face is to go beyond where we are now, to go further. We are pilgrims and we therefore have to make progress. The progression depends upon our willingness to grow, to develop, beyond ourselves, into the profound and generous life of God. So to begin, we sit still.

Then, closing our eyes gently, we begin to recite our mantra. To meditate all we have to do is to say the word from the beginning to the end. Do not think about what you are doing, what you are not doing. Do not think about yourself. Do not wonder 'is this a complete waste of time? What am I going to get out of this?' All those thoughts must fall away, must be abandoned. They will cease to trouble you if you persevere with the mantra, deepening your faith, liberating the power of the Spirit's love. Meditation is continually bringing us to a state of undivided consciousness where we become one with the One who is one. Our growing unity, within ourselves and with God is the process that underlies our sense that we, or rather the life lived in us, is something more profound, more generous, more alive. Meditation asks of us however that we are utterly practical in our commitment, our spiritual commitment.

The call, the destiny that you hear St Paul assign to each of us, is not a call just to enter into the religious moments in our busy schedules, into a bit of spiritual richness. It is to enter fully and utterly, without reserve, without counting the cost, into the truth that empowers each of us to be fully human, truly self-confident, which means confident to love and to be loved. Again, we must remember that we are not talking about some elitist or esoteric doctrine. This call, this destiny, is within the reach of each of us. All we have to do is to begin to commit ourselves to the journey, to the practice. And the practice of this tradition, and do not let anything mislead you on this, is to say the word from the beginning to the end with growing fidelity. This truth of our destiny is not only accessible to us, it is the ground on which all reality stands. To come to this reality we have to learn to be simple, to be still, to be silent. These are the elements of prayer and prayer is to be attentive, attentive to what is the supreme reality of God's presence, his love, within our own hearts. So we must learn to stop thinking about ourselves. We must learn simply to be, which means to be fully attentive in the presence of God, in the presence of the one who is, and who is the ground of our being, and all being. We need have no fear as we set out, as we leave self behind and set out to meet the other. We need have no doubt or fear. The Spirit in our hearts, the Spirit to which we open in meditation is the Spirit of compassion, of gentleness, of forgiveness, of total acceptance, the Spirit of love.

For our lives to be fully human we need to encounter the Spirit of love within ourselves. It is not a journey just for spiritual experts. It is a journey for everyone who would live his or her lives to the full. Who was St Paul writing to when he wrote these words?

> "I pray that your inward eyes may be illumined, so that you may know what is the hope to which he calls you, what the wealth and glory of the share he offers you – and how vast the resources of his power open to us who trust in him." (Eph 1:18–19)

Meditation is the great way of trust. We sit down, we sit still, say our mantra with growing fidelity and trust our whole selves utterly to God. We do that every morning and every evening of our lives and thus we learn to live out of that trust, to live out of the love that faith reveals and liberates.

John Main
from 'The Heart of Creation'

THE LIGHT OF THE WORD

When we talk or think about meditation, it is very easy to get carried away by theory. And meditation is an extremely exciting and wonderful mystery to talk and think about. But the talking and the thinking have a great inbuilt danger, which is that we do not go beyond the words and the ideas and instead remain looking at a reflection in a mirror. We are so fascinated by the reflection and so unaware that the mirror distorts whatever it reflects, that we fail to turn around and see the real thing.

The teaching of a great teacher like John Main has the power to inspire us and to turn around and see the real thing. Seeing the real thing means doing the real thing. It means actually meditating, actually putting in the time, each morning and evening, to see the real thing. The teaching we have received which we try to share and live, is entirely realistic and practical. It is not concerned just with speculation or elaborating theories; it is concerned primarily with experience, experience in faith. First, it is concerned with the experience we all start from when we begin to meditate. Secondly, it is concerned with the experience we pass through as we learn to meditate. Only thirdly is it concerned with the experience we enter into, the goal we arrive at. Because of that intimate connection between the teaching and our own experience, the teaching itself has the authority to reflect and guide our experience. This is what we call a "living tradition".

Each of us enters into it when we begin to meditate. Because it is a tradition that began a long time ago, it is one that has to a great degree formed us into who we are when we come into it. That teaching, that tradition, is simplicity itself. It says that to meditate we must become silent and still, not just externally, not just physically, though these are essential dimensions, but interiorly silent, interiorly still. In this way the tradition leads us to enter the knowledge of unity with ourselves. The teaching leads us to find ourselves. Our exterior stillness reflects the interior stillness. When we meditate we must try to sit as still as possible and not get careless about this discipline of stillness as the weeks and months pass. It may seem a very elementary thing to do but it is the first step, and the first step is all-important. Then you begin to say your mantra. During the time of your meditation you have nothing else to do, nothing else to worry about, nothing to be ambitious about, to plan or to analyze. You have only to say your word. Saying your word will lead you into the ever profounder silence in which you find you can be who you are and (even more wonderful) allow God to be who God is within you.

Whatever thoughts, ideas or images may float across your mind just let them float away. Whatever great insights may come to you just let them go too. Whatever trivial thoughts or distractions may come to you just let them go. It doesn't matter what comes into your mind or what you imagine; simply return to the saying of your word. Repetition purifies. The mantra will purify your heart, your consciousness, and bring you to that pure simplicity of a child, which we need if we are going to enter the Kingdom. The mantra is the way.

When most of us begin the way, our initial experience is very different from what we are eventually led to. It is not one of joy, peace and contentment. We hear this teaching of how to live out of the spring of joy within us. We set out to find the realm of peace within us. Probably, to begin with, we are more likely to encounter restless desire and discontentment. We are all radically discontented because we are encouraged and trained to live so much in the future, planning for the future, or in the past, regretting or analyzing it over and over again. Our restlessness makes us miss the only opportunity we have for contentment, for fullness of life. The only chance we have is the present moment. Missing that we miss everything.

Living in the past or the future we end up discontented, because in being so concerned about what we lack, so preoccupied with what we desire, we fail to see what we have been given. Unless we change this attitude and turn around from the mirror, we are condemned to being discontented. Even when we do get what we desire from time to time, we will still be discontented. Getting what we desire will not satisfy us, because in that concupiscent frame of mind there will always be something else to want beyond our immediate reach. The state of discontent is ruled not by the spirit of love but by egotism. The only way into peace is to recognize and receive what we have been given. The greatest gift that we have been given usually misses our attention. We usually fail to see it. It is not health, wealth, beauty or talent. The greatest gift is our being, simply that we are. This is the first and fundamental gift. If we fail to recognize that, which also means failure to accept it, then nothing that comes our way will really be ours either. Accepting that gift is the first step, the essential step, to becoming fully alive and therefore fully content.

Accepting the gift is what we do when we meditate. Meditation is concerned with being rather than doing, although this is something it takes us a long time to become familiar with as an idea and even longer to accept as experience. It is very difficult for us to be concerned with being rather than with doing. For a while, after we begin to meditate we still regard our meditation as being primarily concerned with doing. We have to recognize this as how we begin. But our perception is purified as we continue. As we learn how to be, how to accept the gift of our being, we find real contentment. We leave behind desire, restlessness and all the images that those passions create. As a result, of course, our doing is itself radically purified by our meditation. The way we live, the quality of our life, the generosity of our relationships, are all in time transformed by the new understanding we learn by learning to be and by accepting the gift of our being.

All that is a process of growth in our spirit. It is not an instant experience. That is why when we begin to meditate it is important not to look for experiences, certainly not to try to engineer or simulate them, to anticipate or possess them. It is a process of growth which is similar to the gradual settling of impurities in a glass of water. At first all the impurities swirl around making the water cloudy, opaque. But if you don't interfere with the glass and if you allow it to stand still and the impurities to settle, the water itself becomes still and so translucently clear. As you look through the water you realize how beautiful is its purity, its clarity and you see what simplicity really is. When it is opaque the water reflects. When it is clear you see through it.

The first thing we have to learn to do is to allow ourselves to settle, to be still. We are all of us cloudy. We are all too self-reflective. We have to allow our consciousness to become clarified. This is the simplifying process of meditation, becoming still at the centre of our being. This means really still, not just thinking about being still or saying how nice it would be if we were still and more spiritual, but in fact being still and in time allowing all our action to flow from harmony with that stillness. In stillness our spirit clarifies. It becomes pure and translucent. The God whose spirit dwells within us then shines through our spirit as sunlight shines through the water. This is what we call purity of heart. This is the clarity of consciousness that allows us to see God. "Blessed are the pure of heart," said Jesus, "for they shall see God".

Kierkegaard defined purity of heart as desiring one thing. Most of us desire too many things. Restricting our desire to one thing gradually purifies us of desire. It clarifies us, because when we meditate all we desire is to say our mantra. Everything else is left behind. Saying our word faithfully, simply and lovingly, brings us to that stillness where we see the light clearly both within and around us. Therefore we see everything clearly because we see it in the light which is the very medium of vision. The psalmist praised God by singing: "In your light we see light."

This clarity is felt as joy. Seeing the light is the essence of joy and so it is the only secure basis of contentment in our life. As the spirit of peace it works for tranquility and harmony in every area of life. It is only necessary that we do become still, then that we stay on the path that leads us further into the stillness. The path only asks us to be totally simple at those two periods of meditation each day and to be as faithful as we can to the saying of our word.

The Light we find is the light of the Word described in the Gospel of John: "When all things began, the Word already was. The Word dwelt with God, and what God was the Word was. The Word, then, was with God at the beginning, and through him all things came to be; no single thing was created without him. All that came to be was alive with his life, and that life was the Light of men. The light shines on in the dark, and the darkness has never mastered it". (John 1 :1–5)

Laurence Freeman from 'Light Within'

"WE ARE WHAT WE DO WITH SILENCE"

St Augustine said quite a few wonderful things and one of them is this: "The whole purpose of life is to restore to health the eye of the heart through which we see God." This is really the whole purpose of prayer as well: to restore to health the eye of the heart through which we see God in ourselves, in one another, in all things. There's a built-in implication in Augustine's description that while the eye of the heart is a gift from God, WE have to work to maintain its health. WE, each of us, are responsible. And there's the sense that the health of the eye of the heart is something that has to be cared for, cultivated, protected against things that challenge it in the course of life, things that assail it both from within and without. And again this is such a terribly vital responsibility, because it is only through this eye that we can truly see God in ourselves, in one another, in all things.

Not through the empirical eye of the senses. Not through the rational eye of the mind or intellect. But through the spiritual eye of the heart. And the more we grow in spirit, the keener and more sustained the vision of this eye, this sight of the spirit. And the greater our love.

So what I'd like to share with you this morning is an ancient way of spiritual growth, a way of spiritual health that's incredibly simple and incredibly powerful. This is the way of contemplative prayer or of meditation, a daily personal discipline, a practice of silence, stillness and simplicity available to each of us, not as a substitute for all the other forms of prayer, but as a center for them. Like the hub of a wheel centers the spokes and makes possible the wheel's motion and stability.

It's important to realize that this way of prayer is deeply rooted in our own Christian tradition, in the gospels and in the teachings of the Early Fathers. But while the roots are deep and still living, the vine has not exactly flourished over the centuries. In fact it's almost been lost and in the organized church is effectively absent, not only not remembered and not taught, but misunderstood, imagined to be foreign, from someone else's tradition like the Buddhists. Or it's seen as a very rarified way, only suitable in our tradition to a very few odd folks hanging around 14th century monasteries in habits and hoods. Certainly not the stuff of everyday Christian men and women like you and like me.

But the good news is that one of the most significant developments in the last 50 years has been the recovery of this tradition in the West, as a truly Christian way of spirituality, and as a way for anyone, for each of us.

One of the people most responsible for this recovery was an English Benedictine monk named John Main, born in 1926 and died in 1982. John Main was, and through his books and tapes remains, a great teacher of contemplative prayer who saw prayer as the primary means of spiritual health, spiritual growth. He had in many ways an extremely practical approach. He didn't promise mystical experiences or visions. He didn't say you would begin to levitate and hear voices. He simply said you would grow in Christ. And he said you could measure that growth not in the quality of your prayer but in the quality of your life, the quality of your love. Only in our daily lives do we find the true fruits or measures of growth in Christ. In fact he said there were five signs:

- greater rootedness in self (the true self, not the false self of the ego)
- deeper emotional stability
- greater intellectual simplicity and clarity
- greater capacity to center on others and away from self
- becoming more loving and more aware of love as the essential energy of life.

Now when John Main talked about the centrality of prayer he wasn't talking about the quality and quantity of our petitions or intercessions. By how much we said and how often we said it. He was talking about the quality and the quantity of our silence, our capacity to be still and silent and simple in the presence of God for a sustained period of time each and every day. He was talking about the prayer of the heart, the prayer not of words and images, but of silence. Which brings us to the title of this talk.

It comes from a 19th century German, Friedrich von Hugel, who wrote a book probably none of us has on our nightstands at the moment called *The Mystical Elements of Religion*. Von Hugel came up with a startlingly clear declaration of the end and means of spiritual life, as well as a practicum of prayer, all in seven words. He said, "We are what we do with silence."

We are what we do with silence. Von Hugel's definition poses a curious alternative to the more familiar definitions of this sort, like the ever popular: we are what we eat. Actually, variations on this line could provide a matchbook history of human philosophy, if you will, from we are who our parents were, we are what we think, we are what we produce, we are what we buy, we are what our brain chemistry happens to be at the moment.

So, how strange a notion of Von Hugel's: we are what we do with silence. It seems totally opposed to everything that otherwise would define our success and identity. And yet his claim echoes at the heart of every spiritual tradition, every wisdom tradition on earth, especially ours. But in the Christian tradition, the practice and purpose of silence, the wisdom of silence, has been all but lost, not just in the institutional settings of prayer but for personal prayer as well. We may sit in external silence as we pray, but inside we may be talking up a storm. And in church because there is so little external silence, interior silence is virtually impossible.

There is most certainly in our commercial, competitive culture a great aversion to silence. Instead of silence, stillness and simplicity we have distraction and complexity, we have noise and busyness. There's chatter of every kind, but maybe the most deafening is the chatter that takes place within our own minds, what the Buddhists call our monkey minds, each a tree of monkeys, all chattering at once.

Obviously this is a long story, but the point for now is that if what we do with silence is run from it, avoid it at all costs, stuff it full of noise and busyness, preoccupy it with our worries and fantasies, with ourselves: WE CANNOT GROW IN SPIRIT. And we don't. We can't fully live in the present moment, the only moment we ever truly have.

Let me tell you a little Buddhist story about two Zen disciples that illustrates the point. Each of these disciples was bragging about the relative merits of his respective master. The first disciple said: My master stands on one side of the river and I stand on the other holding a piece of paper. He draws a picture in the air and the picture appears on my paper! He works miracles!! The second disciple was unimpressed. My master works greater miracles than that:

> "When he sleeps, he sleeps
> When he eats, he eats
> When he works, he works
> When he meditates, he meditates."

So what is this greater miracle the second disciple describes? It's the greater miracle of knowing how to simply be, to simply be in the present moment, fully mindful, fully present. So what's so miraculous about that? Obviously for creatures who are usually so thoroughly distracted, so terribly self-conscious, so often lost in the past or lost in the future, so often performing and living in the eyes of others, the simple sanctity of the moment, of the Now, is pretty miraculous. The second master's ability to simply be, and in the last line, to be still and silent and simple in meditation or prayer is indeed the greater miracle.

And this is very consistent with the wisdom tradition of our own faith. We have Christ's own admonitions on prayer in Matthew: "Go to your secret place and shut the door" do not babble on. We have powerful witness early on, especially in the wisdom of the Desert Fathers, who in the first few hundred years after Christ, sought to live purely and honestly in accord with the gospel of Jesus in the deserts of Africa. As many of you know, the Sayings of the Desert Fathers, simple short aphorisms without analysis or interpretation represent a treasure chest of insight that still sparkles. Here's one of the Sayings that most fits our theme today:

A certain brother went to see Abbot Moses and said, "Father can you give me a good word?" Abbot Moses said to him, "Go, sit in your cell and your cell will teach you everything."

Or as the Psalmist said a thousand years before, "Be still and know that I am God." And if we need a more current rendition, we could try the great French aphorist philosopher, Pascal, who said, "All the troubles of life come upon us because we refuse to sit quietly for a while each day in our room."

The Christian tradition of teaching stillness, silence, and simplicity as the central way of prayer is a powerful and enduring one, even if most of us never had the chance to encounter it in the regular course of religious education. Perhaps the most pivotal figure in the western contemplative tradition is John Cassian, the 5th century student of the Desert Fathers and the great teacher of St Benedict, whose rule still constitutes the spiritual foundation of Anglican faith.

As a young man, Cassian goes to Egypt with a companion to learn from the Fathers and his subsequent writings formed the core of the western monastic tradition. Here's a sample of Cassian's insight. The gospel reminds us, he says, to enter into our chamber and shut the door and pray to our Father. OK so what does that really mean? This is how Cassian translates the metaphor and applies it to our personal experience.

"We pray within our chamber, when removing our hearts inwardly from the din of all thoughts and anxieties, we disclose our prayer in secret and in closest intercourse to the Lord. We pray with closed doors when with closed lips and complete silence we pray to the searcher not of words but of hearts."

'The searcher not of words but of hearts.' The Father who already knows what we need before we ask him. The Spirit who prays in us, because as the gospel reminds us, "we do not know how to pray."

But the great practical insight Cassian offers is the actual HOW. He shared what he called the "formula" of repeating a single verse or short phrase: sit down, sit still, say your word, repeat your word, not as a magic incantation, but as a tool to help you to be humble and still before God. A means through which we might experience the "poverty of spirit", Jesus describes in the Beatitudes. Here's what Cassian says about the formula for contemplative prayer, the humble repetition of a single verse or word:

"The mind should unceasingly cling to it until, strengthened by constant use and by continual meditation, it casts off and rejects the rich and full material of all manner of thoughts. It restricts itself to the poverty of this one verse and so arrives with ready ease at that beatitude of the gospel which hold the first place among the other beatitudes: for he says "Blessed are the poor in spirit, for theirs is the kingdom of heaven." And so one becomes grandly poor."

The poverty of one verse. Being grandly poor in spirit before God. These are the words which fueled John Main's rediscovery of this tradition in the mid-twentieth century.

The tradition of the teaching from Cassian to Main is built on the notion that silence is not just the absence of noise, but a practice, a discipline, a choice, a way of being. A way of humility. A way of Faith. The tradition also declares that the secret, what we seek, often so desperately, is not out there. It's within. It's the treasure buried in our own hearts. But to discover it, to fully encounter and experience the secret, we must learn how to be still, simple, and silent in some sort of regular disciplined way.

So what is this gift that we already have? What's the treasure buried in our hearts? Fr John says it's the peace of Christ himself, his parting gift to each one of us, a peace out of which we can live and go forth each day, if we can only be in touch with it. This is of course the theology of the indwelling Christ and the theology of meditation in the Christian tradition. Let's go to the evening of the day of the resurrection and read in John:

> "Then the same day at evening, being the first day of the week, when the doors were shut for fear of the Jews, where the disciples were assembled. Jesus came and stood in the midst and said to them, Peace be with you. And he showed them his hands and his side. The disciples were glad when they saw the Lord and so Jesus said to them again, Peace to you. As the Father has sent Me, I also send you. And when He had said this, He breathed on them and said to them: Receive the Holy Spirit."

The tradition of prayer inspired by our faith in the risen Christ who lives and lives in us, is not then a long distance phone call but an entry into our own hearts. It's not a gift you have to save up for or worry about when it will arrive. As Fr Laurence Freeman, the Benedictine successor of John Main, reminds us, "It has already happened. The Spirit has already been breathed into our hearts."

It is this spirit and its power of recognition and love that Jesus has breathed into every human heart. It is the central gift of our faith. What we're talking about is prayer, the actual practice of prayer. Again, not the prayer where we're asking for something or thinking about ourselves or others. But the prayer of the heart where we are simply being and being simple in the presence of God. Where we're not trying to prove anything or impress anyone. Where we're still trying, despite all the frenzy and clamor and complexity of our lives, to "be still and know that (God) is God".

So that's the tradition. A spiritual discipline, a way of prayer that doesn't replace the other forms of prayer. But a way of prayer that grounds us in the most important work that Jesus asks us to do: Leave self behind. And why? That we might be sanctimonious, holier than thou, strange misfits? No. So that we might grow in love, so that we might truly see God in ourselves, in others, in all things.

It's simply a matter of paying attention to what you do with your silence. Reserve at least 20 minutes at the beginning and end of each day. Reserve this time despite everything else you do. Reserve it just to be: to be quiet, to be still, to be simple. Try to find as quiet a place as possible. Use the same space if you can and make it sacred. Light a candle. Use an icon. Take off your shoes. (Don't even think about turning on a radio!) Sit down and be comfortable. Keep your spine straight. And close your eyes lightly. Don't move. Stay as still as you possibly can. But don't clench up. Relax but stay alert. And just be. Just breathe.

Breathe in the Holy Spirit Christ has given you and continues to give you. Take just a minute to concentrate on the miracle of your breath, on its ever-renewing gift. And then as the tradition teaches us, begin to say a single sacred word, silently, interiorly. John Main calls it the "mantra". The word John Main recommends is Maranatha, an Aramaic word, Jesus' own language, which means "Come, Lord" or "The Lord comes". Say it as four syllables of equal length: Ma-ra-na-tha.

Say it gently and continuously, from the beginning to the end of your prayer period. Don't think about anything. Just say the word gently and in faith. Thoughts and distractions will come, but let them pass. Don't go with them. Accept the word as a gift to help bring your mind to focus and attention, to the simple and still prayer of the heart.

Let me end with these words of Fr Laurence Freeman, who reminds us of the purpose of our prayer is, as St Augustine said, "to restore to health the eye of the heart". And who reminds us that prayer is personal work, a daily discipline, that takes time, devotion, love, and faith.

> "Growth in spirit is not an instant experience. It is a process similar to the gradual settling of the impurities in a glass of water. At first all the impurities swirl around making the water cloudy, opaque. But if you don't interfere with the glass and if you allow it to stand still and the impurities to settle, the water itself becomes still and so translucently clear. As you look through the water you realize how beautiful is its purity, its clarity, and you see what simplicity really is. When it is opaque the water reflects. When it is clear, you see through it."

The first thing we have to learn to do is to allow ourselves to settle, to be still. We are all of us cloudy. We are all too self-reflective. We have to allow our consciousness to become clarified. This is the simplifying process of meditation, become still at the pure center of our being. This means really still, not just thinking about being still or saying how nice it would be if we were still and more spiritual, but in fact being still and in time allowing all our action to flow from harmony with that stillness. In stillness our spirit clarifies. It becomes pure and translucent. The God whose Spirit dwells within us then shines through our spirit as sunlight shines through the water. This is what we call purity of heart. This is the clarity of consciousness that allows us to see God.

Carla Cooper

FROM CASSIAN TO MAIN: MEDITATION AND THE CHRISTIAN TRADITION

The title of this talk is "From Cassian to Main", but it could just as easily be "From Main to Cassian". This is so because we can't learn about John Main's personal journey to meditation without learning about John Cassian's own journey. These two journeys, one at the very beginning of the tradition and the other during our lifetime, are key moments in what Fr Laurence calls "the living line". This living line is not an accumulation of theory or doctrine. It's a history of real persons who searched for and found a way to pray and a way to be.

Fr John told his own story quite beautifully in the very first book he published on meditation, *The Gethsemani Talks*. Based on talks he gave in 1976 at the invitation of the monks of the Abbey of Gethsemani in Kentucky, this little book remains one of the very best introductions to meditation in the Christian tradition. It captures with simplicity and authority Fr John's discovery of the contemplative root of Christianity, a discovery he shared with extraordinary results.

The book charts for us very briefly some of the key milestones in the unfolding of the tradition, from the 4th century Desert Fathers and Mothers in the wilderness of Egypt and Palestine; to John Cassian who imported the Desert Wisdom to the West in the early 5th century; to the development of western monasticism through Cassian's foremost pupil, St Benedict and his Rule, promulgated widely in the 6th century; to the anonymous and amazing *Cloud of Unknowing* in the late 14th century; to the English Benedictine Augustine Baker's *Holy Wisdom* in the 17th century, and so on. Through all this time, the Eastern Church kept contemplative practice at the center of the church, by nurturing the prayer of the heart, the Jesus Prayer. And, of course, that tradition's repository of wisdom, *The Philokalia*, remains a great and constant companion for our journey.

John Main's own rediscovery of the tradition began when he was introduced to the practice of meditation and the mantra in Malaya during his stint in the Foreign Service in the mid-50s. It was a practice he was discouraged to pursue after he became a monk at Ealing Abbey in 1959, for the reason that such a practice was foreign and not part of the Christian tradition. He described the ensuing period as a desert. It was not until the early 70s when Fr John was serving as Headmaster of St Anselm's, a Benedictine school in Washington, D.C. that he was able to verify the Christian roots of meditation and the practice of the mantra. He came back, he said, on God's terms, not his own.

As a way of trying to help a young visitor answer questions about the history of Christian mysticism, Main was drawn back to Baker's *Holy Wisdom*. And here he found a way back to the wellspring of the tradition in John Cassian. Fr John wrote that Baker's "frequent reminder of the emphatic insistence St Benedict lays on Cassian's Conferences sent me to them seriously for the first time". And it was here in the conferences that he wrote, "I arrived home once more and returned to the practice of the mantra" and meditation.

Reading these still extraordinarily fresh conferences ourselves, we can share just a little of the joy and relief that John Main must have experienced as he sought to anchor his own intuition and insight deeply in the Christian tradition. What I would like to do here is to summarize briefly some of the key points of affinity between Cassian and Main, explain a little about Cassian's background and experience, and then look more closely at Conferences Nine and Ten, the conferences on prayer, which you have read in preparation for this School.

For John Main, Cassian provided both a Christocentric theology of prayer that is absolutely rooted in the Gospels and a practicum of prayer, the how to. More than anything, he made prayer clearly a matter of personal experience and personal discipline, not a matter of theory or doctrine. Cassian brought to his discussion of prayer the existential authority of one who prays; a real person who really prays.

For Cassian, both the theology and the practice of prayer are rooted in the central Christian truth that God is and dwells within us (through the Holy Spirit which Christ has given us), and the central Christian paradox: we must lose our life to find it. As John Main understood, it's not "a person must lose his life", it's you who must lose your life. I must lose my life. And that is not just the ultimate loss of death, but also the daily sacrifice of all that is self-bound, the need to give back the "possessions" which were never really "ours" in the first place. It is the leaving behind of self that Jesus says is necessary if we are to follow him. Similarly, we must also lose our prayer to find it, lose the comfortable tradition, the familiar images, the piety, and the self-concern. But what we find instead, in the silence and solitude and stillness of meditation, is the most beautiful fruit of prayer: poverty of spirit.

This is not poverty in the sense of destitution or absence. It is poverty in the sense that there is really only one thing to know: the presence of God within us. This is a condition of simplicity that demands, as Mother Julian says, nothing less than everything. It is, as Thomas Merton has described, "a clear unobstructed vision of the truth", an intuitive grasp of (who and what we really are) ... not what the false self lures us to imagine. It is recognition that by ourselves we are nothing, that only in God through Christ, do we live and move and have our true being.

Fr John said that it is out of the reality of this poverty that we "pass over". He said that for Cassian the spiritual journey was a passover – from sorrow to joy, isolation to community, fear to love, from false self to true self. And the vehicle for that journey is our prayer. So the poverty, according to Cassian, becomes a Grand Poverty because it gives us the truth, the simple gift of simply being, being in the presence of the Love that floods our hearts.

CASSIAN'S BACKGROUND

While we don't have much definitive information about John Cassian's early life, he was born in 360 to a well-to-do family living, most likely, in what is now Romania. He spent the last years of his life in Marseilles. This is where he wrote his great works, including the Conferences, and where he died in the early 430s. In between the well-born youth and the prolific old age, were the extraordinary experiences in Palestine, Egypt, Constantinople, Rome, that shaped his life and teaching: teachings through which he set the course of western monasticism and laid the groundwork for the contemplative tradition we practice today.

In keeping with his genteel origins, Cassian was well educated and studied the Classics, but he was clearly a seeker after God. Sometime in his twenties he left family and possessions behind, journeying with his friend Germanus to Bethlehem where they joined an established monastery "in search", as John Main describes it, "of a living tradition" of life in Christ. Instead, they suffered what Cassian described as "grievous loss from the mediocrity of the manner of life there". Still seeking a better way, Cassian sought his Abbot's permission to visit the monasteries located in the deserts of Egypt.

There in the desert Cassian and Germanus found not more institutionalized mediocrity, but a practice of faith and a way of life so fresh and so consonant with the gospels that they remained, not for the few months the Abbot gave them permission for, but for more than 10 years. Here in the deserts of Skete, and deeper into Nitrea, where at the peak of the movement more than 5000 monks lived in caves and huts across the Nitrean Valley, they found the first Christian hermits, whom we know as the Desert Fathers and Mothers. And among the many were the great elders, the abbas and ammas, including Abba Isaac, whose lucid and uncompromising teaching on prayer forms the heart and culminating wisdom of Cassian's Conferences.

Cassian and Germanus made one appeal to Isaac: tell us about prayer, unceasing prayer. John Main described them as listening with growing rapture as the holy man spoke, realizing that "at last we have found our teacher". "As they listened their hearts burned within them as he spoke of ceaseless prayer. And their response was wholehearted: This is what we must do!"

While it's obvious that Cassian's personal experience with the Desert Teachers was the single most influential source of the Conferences, there is no other source for Desert Wisdom than the Gospels themselves. Indeed the best way to capture the essence of Desert Wisdom and Isaac's discourse is to go back to the teachings of Jesus on prayer, especially in the Gospel of Matthew. Jesus says in the Sermon on the Mount that our prayer must not be merely outward. It's not about appearing holy. It is about learning the courage of solitude in our "private room", in the inmost depths of our hearts. Prayer is interior. It is not about "babbling on", since God knows what we need before we ask him. It is not about seeking personal or material well being, not about indulging in self-centered anxiety. It is about setting our minds and hearts, in loving attention, on God's kingdom first and always.

There is perhaps no greater distillation of the Desert way of life, its humility, simplicity, charity, its aversion to piety, pretension and self-consciousness, its hesitancy to judge and scorn than the life of Jesus himself and the great teaching in Matthew 6. And there is no clearer foundation for the practice of meditative prayer and the example of Poverty of Spirit that Isaac shares with Cassian and which Cassian shares with all who encounter these beautiful Conferences, John Main in the 1960s, and you and me today.

THE CONFERENCES THEMSELVES

Let's look briefly, but more closely, at these two Conferences themselves. Again the desert setting is compelling; we can imagine the two young pilgrims at the feet of the elder. Isaac begins Conference Nine with a paradox about prayer – so we know we're off to a good start. It's the paradox of perseverance and tranquility: doing and being, trying and letting go, effort and grace. Basically he says there's a reciprocal and inseparable relation between the two. In a little parable of prayer (and, of course, life), he says, you can't have peace unless you work at it and you can't work at it unless you have peace.

The key, as always, is humility: approaching prayer not as a personal achievement, but as a simple act of faith. One of the things any reader notices immediately about Isaac's description is his amazing and astonishingly modern grasp of the human experience. There's not an emotion, a mood, a tendency he leaves out, as he describes the struggle to achieve purity of heart through prayer. He goes on in Chapter 5 to outline the special dangers, the distractions and temptations that keep us from the simple practice of prayer. He doesn't just list the obvious faults like lust or blasphemy; he gives a far more sophisticated analysis of those things that often masquerade as virtues, especially what we might call the "Vanity of Doing", with all our self-conscious, self-centered distractions buzzing around that vanity.

Isaac continues his discourse by identifying the four basic types of prayer: supplication, vows and promises, intercession, and thanksgiving. He says the prayer that combines all of these is, of course, the Lord's Prayer and does a very nice line by-line-explication, culminating in the pivotal reminder in Chapter 24 that the prayer is not about you. It "contains no request for riches, no allusion to honors, no demand for power and strength, no mention of bodily health or temporal existence". But Isaac's key point in this description of prayer is that there is still a loftier stage: what he calls in Chapter 25 the "wordless prayer that transcends all human understanding and is distinguished not by voice or tongue or word".

Later, Isaac concludes this discussion in Chapter 35 with one of the loveliest passages of all: "Before anything else, we must carefully observe the Gospel command which says that we should go into our room and pray with the door shut." And here's how we fulfill that command: "We pray in our room when we withdraw our hearts completely from the clatter of every thought and concern. We pray with the door shut when, with closed lips and in total silence, we pray to the searcher not of words but of hearts."

This is, of course, a beautiful conclusion to Conference Nine, but as our boys realize it's a little short on the how. How do we get there from here? So it's back to Isaac for Conference Ten. Cassian gives Conference Ten tremendous dramatic shape and intensity, setting the stage for the second meeting with Abba Isaac with a telling little desert vignette. It so happens that Cassian and Germanus are visiting at the time of Epiphany. And one of the traditions of Epiphany is sending out from Alexandria, the state capital of the Desert, a Festal Letter announcing the date of Easter and delivering a little message. It so happens that the subject of this year's message is the heresy of Anthropomorphism, which envisions God in the form of man because man was made in the image of God. The letter, Cassian points out, was not very well accepted and wasn't even read aloud in other communities, the one our friends are visiting is the exception.

It so happens that in this community lives a venerable old monk named Serapion who outstrips everyone in virtue and holiness. Hardly a scholar, he is a very simple monk who has lived a very simple life of devotion. As the letter is read aloud, the monks hear about the incomprehensive nature of God never to be apprehended by eye or conceived by mind. The old monk is greatly shaken. He hears the message and accepts the truth, but Oh the pain. Bewildered and abandoned, he bursts into tears and cries out at the end of Chapter 3, "They have taken my God from me. I have no one to hold onto, no one to worship, no one to speak to".

And so with this very poignant backdrop, Cassian and Germanus make their way back to Isaac. Isaac speaks to them of the incident they have all just witnessed with great sympathy and compassion. He uses it as an example of the maturation, almost always painful, that we all must pass through if we are to say with the Apostle: "If we have known Christ after the flesh, yet now we know Him so no more." And just as we must leave self behind to find our true self, we must leave "our God" behind. And we must leave "our prayer" behind as well. Isaac goes on to underscore the fact that prayer is not about fixating or grasping onto an image, it's about getting beyond all images. It's about purity of heart, the state in which we are emptied and open to God. Not a god as a thing "out there", but as a reality within God who dwells in us.

In Chapter 7 Isaac goes to the most powerful example of all, the prayer of Jesus in John's Gospel. The truth is that we do share in the same spirit, the same love. We are "so united to Him", Isaac says, "that whatever we breathe or think or speak is God". We can't find without what is within, and we can't find what is within without stripping away all that is false. Our life already is continuous prayer; the Spirit has already been breathed into our hearts. To know this we only have to stop and look and see.

Germanus then occupies the entire 250 lines of the 8th Chapter with one question that can be distilled into one word: How? Isaac offers in the 9th chapter (mercifully only 12 lines long) an astute response that basically says I cannot really tell you the right answer until you have the savvy to ask the right question. And so in Chapter 10 we get down to the nitty gritty. There is something that you can do, he says. And so he introduces the formula of continual prayer, a teaching he says was delivered to him by the oldest Fathers and only divulged to a few. That's not because it's so difficult or hard to master, but only the few have the purity of heart and courage of humility to receive it. It's not about being smart or well born. It's about humility.

The method he offers is to use a single phrase. The one he recommends is from the psalm: "Oh God, come to my assistance; Lord, make haste to help me." The single phrase is not a magical incantation, it is merely a tool against distraction; "a coat of mail, a strong shield", he says. We don't have to worry about what it says, because it contains all things. And because God already knows all things, our job is not to tell him anything. Our job is, in simplicity and faith, to empty ourselves of ourselves, of the detail and distraction of self that occludes the simple, living truth. And so in the practice of the poverty of one verse, we become "grandly poor", in unity with the God who is love and who lives in all.

Germanus and Cassian are happy to hear about all this, but they're still impatient. Germanus' questions at the end of Conference Ten remind us of Fr John asking his teacher in Malaya: How long will this take? What can I expect? How will this work? The wise Hindu swami, just like the wise Christian Abba, had just one response: Say your word. Do your work. I said it was simple, I didn't say it was easy. Isaac begins with the paradox of persistence and tranquility of effort and gift, responsibility and grace. And, in a way, he ends with it as well. Despite all distractions, we need to persist in the simple faith that the peace of Christ is already within us. But we know we cannot be ever mindful of the gift of that peace, we can't begin to live out of it, unless we persist in our prayer. Say your word. Do your work. Be always mindful of who you truly are in God and who God truly is in you. That, as Father John, says is what you are born for.

Carla Cooper

Sharing the GIFT

The MEDITATION Period

THE MEDITATION PERIOD

Now that the introductory talk is completed, this is the moment to introduce meditation. Be aware that this is a challenge. This is the moment when you are really called upon to share your faith: by saying no more about it!

If the people have been sitting for a long time allow a few moments to stand and stretch or take a five-minute break, while keeping everyone silent. It can be useful to lead a couple of stretching exercises before sitting again if you feel comfortable in doing this. If not, allow a few moments for them to recollect themselves before introducing the meditation

Do not be afraid to take a few moments to help the group to get into the best possible position for the meditation.

Give instructions on how to sit
If you are sitting on a chair sit well into the back of the seat of the chair, then use the back of the chair to guide you rather than to prop you up. The most important rule of posture is that the spine should be upright. Thus you need to ensure that your head, ribcage and pelvis can find their natural alignment over each other. Then you are balanced and do not need to hold yourself up. The crown of the head should be as if drawn up to the ceiling with the chin towards the chest not pointing forwards or up. This allows the back of the neck to be long and free and therefore relaxed.

If you are on the floor or on a prayer stool the same rules apply to the spine. It should be poised and upright, but not strained or tense or rigid. It is important to take time at home to find the best way of sitting.

However you choose to sit, it is important that you do not spend the time of meditation thinking about the pain you are in or the discomfort. The body should be as attuned as possible without being strained or in pain. Your capacity to sit well will grow with the practice. Remember the first step to stillness is sitting still for the time of the meditation.

Now that you are settled take a few moments to feel your body in the chair, be aware of the points of contact with chair or ground. Feel your natural weight resting.

Now become aware of your breathing. Feel the inflow and the outflow of the breath. Our breath is the breath of life. Breath is the same word as spirit in many languages, so being aware of our breathing is very helpful in becoming still. Do not alter your breath, just try to allow your abdomen to move so that the breath flows into the base of the lungs. This abdominal breathing is excellent for health as well as for meditation.

Now close your eyes lightly
When you feel ready, gently introduce your prayer word, your mantra. The mantra we suggest is the word MARANATHA. If you use this word say it slowly as four equally stressed syllables MA - RA - NA - THA.

Other suitable words would be the name of "Jesus" or "Abba". As you say the word, listen to it and allow it to sink from the mind into the heart. Do not think about its meaning. John Main observed that many people say the mantra in time with the rhythm of their breathing or heartbeat. If you can do one or the other, that's fine. However, he said, if you cannot say it naturally to either, then "just say it, as you can". It is important always to use the same word once you have chosen one, so that it can become rooted in your being and say itself there. Do not use the mantra to knock out thoughts or repress feelings. Be very gentle and simply keep returning your attention lightly but faithfully to the word every time you get distracted. Come back without self-blame or criticism.

"We will meditate now for 30 minutes"
Having given the lead in instruction, tell them that the meditation period will begin and end with a couple of minutes of quiet music. This is merely to help them to put aside the words that have been used up until now.

At the end, give them adequate time to come out of the meditation, especially if a question and answer period is to follow. Here it could be useful to warn people always to take adequate time to come out of meditation and to recommend ways of timing the meditation at home. There are tapes available with a selection of pre-recorded music, followed by silence for the meditation time, and then more music signaling the end of the meditation. You may have used one of these to time the meditation or a soft beeper to avoid the distraction of 'watching the clock' during the time of meditation.

Length of time could also be mentioned here, perhaps beginning with 20 minutes and slowly increasing it to 30 minutes, which is the optimum time. Also stress the importance of regularity and twice-daily meditations if one wishes to take up this way of prayer. It is useful to point out that taking up meditation often takes people time. We are always beginning and it takes time to get started. There may be starts and stops. Commitment grows the more we persevere on the path, until it becomes central to our lives.

Sharing the **GIFT**

QUESTIONS
and ANSWERS

QUESTIONS AND ANSWERS

In the discussion period after the meditation session there will probably be a range of questions. Respond as best you can. If you can't think of an answer, just say 'I don't know' or 'I'll think about that'. But more than likely, you can respond very adequately from your own experience and reading, in your own words. The following are merely some frequently asked questions with adequate answers. How would you respond using your own words?

Q. Why do we use a mantra? What is the role of the mantra and how do I choose one?

A. The purpose of the mantra is threefold: first, it helps to deal with distractions. The mind needs a point of focus, something for it to be absorbed in so distractions can be ignored. Secondly, it leads to a condition of simplicity. Thirdly and most importantly for us who meditate as Christians, the saying of the mantra is an expression of faith in Christ who lives in our hearts.

The mantra is chosen with care. It is an expression of our faith. Meditation is Christian because of the faith of the person meditating. The mantra is our expression of this. While it is acceptable to choose your own mantra, in the ideal a teacher gives the student a mantra. The Spirit is the inner teacher, so the inner teacher can inspire a self-chosen mantra.

The mantra that Fr John recommended MARANATHA. It is an Aramaic word, the language Jesus spoke. It means Come Lord or the Lord comes. As it is not in our own language it does not have any thoughts attached to it and does not encourage us to think. It is a balanced rhythmic word, with the long "a" sound. It fits well with the rhythm of the breath and it is one of the oldest Christian prayers. Abba or the name of Jesus or the Jesus prayer or part of it or any short phrase of Scripture can be used as a mantra. The 'formula' that John Cassian recommended was the phrase: "O God come to my aid, O Lord make haste to help me". Choosing your word is important. Once you have chosen it, it is important, in this tradition, to always stay with the same word. Thus it becomes rooted in the heart and becomes a way to praying always.

Q. Is it necessary to meditate twice a day? I find it possible to fit in one period, but the second is often impossible.

A. Once someone complained to Fr John that he could not find time for the second period of meditation. He expected Fr John to sympathize with him. While recognizing that it is not always easy, Fr John's response was simply that if he really wanted it enough he would find the time. The man went home and revised his schedule and found the time. However once is better than not at all, one should do what one can and the commitment will grow with continuing practice.

Q. Is the length of the meditation period important?

A. Yes, you have to give it a fair shot. You can't just take a minute here and a minute there. It's like baking bread; you have to leave it for a sufficient amount of time for it to rise. Twenty minutes is pretty well the minimum amount of time. It takes us almost that length of time to come down to any level of stillness and peace or mental quiet. Thirty minutes is the ideal time but it my take some people a while to build up to a thirty minute period twice a day. What is important is that you set your time and then stick to it. It is a good idea to have an external signal so that you don't have to be looking at your watch. It is also helpful to meditate with others fairly regularly. You will often find that people who begin meditation in extreme situations of their lives, tend to get there pretty quickly. A sense of urgency speeds it up because they want to waste less time.

Q. Is the way of breathing important?

A. The first aim of this form of meditation is to say the mantra continually, and that is what we have to learn to do. We should breathe naturally. Don't concentrate on your breathing. Give all the attention to the mantra. You will find that quite naturally the mantra will integrate itself with your breathing. Sometimes it coordinates with some other bodily rhythm like the pulse or heartbeat. Some people say the mantra to their breathing. A simple way might be to say the mantra as you breathe in, and breathe out in silence. Or "Ma-ra" as you breathe in and "Na-tha" as you breathe out. Learning to breathe well, using the abdomen, is highly recommended for health not only for meditation. Proper breathing is an important aid to relaxation and goes with posture.

Fr John did not stress breathing, as he was concerned to keep the discipline simple and not to emphasize the method too much, because then that gets turned into technique. When you get too interested in technique, you forget the purpose of it.

Q. Is posture important when meditating?

A. Yes. The most important rule of posture is to keep the spine upright. If you use a chair, find one of the right height that gives your back the kind of support it needs. If the spine is held erect and relaxed it is possible to stay alert. Slumped posture leads to drowsiness or even sleep. The ideal posture is the lotus posture as this keeps the spine automatically in its natural upright position. This is not possible for most of us, finding a good posture cross legged on the floor or using a prayer stool can be almost as good. However the most important thing is that you are upright and alert without being in unnecessary pain or discomfort. A physical practice like yoga can help greatly with both posture and breathing. Because meditation involves the whole person, body, psyche and spirit, what we do with our body during meditation is of very great importance and learning to sit well is a vital ingredient in learning to move deeper into the silence, stillness and simplicity of meditation.

Q. I like to meditate but it is a very private thing for me. Why should I meditate with a group? It is distracting for me. Why should I go to a group?

A. It is important to meditate on one's own and most of the time this is our situation. However many people find it difficult to keep up regularly on their own, especially in hard times. John Main believed in the importance of the community that meditation creates. The silence in a group can often be deeper than when we are alone. The group gives support and encourages people to keep on practicing on their own. People who meditate together find the experience bonds them to each other at a deep level even when they do not know much about each other. Thus groups have all these functions, but there are some people who do practice regularly on their own without the support of a group. They also know that whenever they meditate they are never alone, but are united to all other meditators around the world.

Q. How is this different from other forms of meditation, like Transcendental Meditation, or prayer? How does meditation help us to relate to other people?

A. The answer to both questions is "unity". First of all it is important to see what meditation, in the Christian tradition we are talking about, shares in common with other traditions as well as how it may differ. The unity in meditation is more important for us to reflect on. But what makes meditation different as a spiritual practice is that it is not practiced as a technique. There is a world of difference between meditating as a technique and as a discipline. We are technologically conditioned and so we think that it is a great technique to discover. We think, "I will use this and see what I get out of it, improve my performance, and I can let go of it if it does not help". But as a discipline we bring a dimension of faith and perseverance to meditation. Perhaps we have to practice for some time before we really understand what that faith means. But this is why it is important that meditation is taught as a spiritual discipline rather than a technique because, to put it crudely, you're more likely to get the best results from it as a spiritual discipline, simply because you are more likely to persevere. With faith as your motive force there is more reason to persevere.

What makes meditation Christian is your Christian faith. It isn't the technique that makes it Christian, Buddhist or Hindu. It is the faith you bring to it. That is why it is such a marvelous way for each person, whatever their faith, to fulfill their faith journey and personally verify the truths of their faith while at the same time sharing deeply a spiritual experience with people of other faiths. The terrible error is saying, "well, I believe in my faith, and that means that somebody else's faith must be wrong". Logically, intellectually that is where we get stuck. But at the level of the spirit we experience unity, and unity is what meditation leads us to. This becomes quite a perceptible reality as you meditate in a group. You don't communicate through language or through the body when you meditate. But there is a deeper communication at work. You will find too that when you have meditated with someone you relate to them quite differently and more easily, from a deeper level of personal unity.

Q. Do some people come to meditation without being taught?

A. Yes, they do. In teaching meditation you can make it sound as if the mantra is something that has just been discovered. But it is a very natural conclusion to certain states of consciousness that people enter naturally: that we do restrict our consciousness to one word and that one word leads on to full silence.

Q. When I meditate I get a tingling sensation in my hands, is this all right? (A thumping heart, feelings of heat or cold or any other physical sensation)

A. When we are meditating the integration and harmonizing of our whole person is gradually taking place. This is positive, sometimes it takes the form of various physical sensations, these simply need to be ignored and they will pass when they have done their work. These sensations are connected with the movement and flow of energy through our system. The relaxation created by meditation allows the energy in us to flow more freely and this can cause physical sensations.

Q. When I meditate I see color, this is very pleasant should I enjoy it? (This can be light or sensations of love, peace etc)

A. The important things to remember is that none of the experiences we may have along the way are the goal of meditation. They are all part of the integration process. The vital thing is not to become attached to them, or desire them, but to just allow them to come and go and continue to pay attention to your mantra.

Q. I have been meditating for some time, but it seems to be making me worse! I often experience a lot of anger when I meditate. At other times I feel very sad and cry a lot. What is happening?

A. When we meditate we have to pass through all the layers of our consciousness, as we move towards God in the depth of our being. There is no way to the depth of union with God except through the layers of our being. Actually what you experience is the healing of your emotions. It may not feel like this when you are experiencing it, but it is the release of old wounds, grief etc. Again the important thing is to try to just allow things to release, as it were allow the firework display, while you gently try to keep your focus on your mantra. At times the pain or other emotion becomes intolerable then you may need to seek some help or advise or counseling outside the time of meditation. Other outlets can also be sought such as painting, writing, etc. Whatever other helps you need at times like this keep meditating. The combination of meditation and other forms of healing work can be very powerful.

Q. I find that sometimes in the meditation, I am saying the mantra and I become at peace and it seems to me, at that moment that the appropriate thing to do is to stop saying the mantra and to remain at peace. If I continue to say the mantra at that moment, I am interfering with this open window of peace. I am forcing my head to keep thinking. What is your teaching on this?

A. John Main taught that at a certain point, maybe after many years, the mantra would lead us into complete silence, maybe just for very brief moments, during the period of meditation. But this is an experience, which we should neither anticipate nor desire. What does complete silence mean? You are not in complete silence if you are able to say "I am silent" or "I am resting" or "I am enjoying this". Then you are already thinking. This is a very subtle, but essential part of the teaching.

Saying the mantra continuously leads to a change in the way you say the mantra. Over the weeks, months, years you say the mantra with less effort, less force, it becomes more faithful, but also more gentle. John Main said that at first we say the mantra in the head with effort; then we sound it in the heart with greater ease and greater self-acceptance of the distractions; and then we listen to the mantra with wholehearted attention. When seen in this way saying the mantra is not thinking, it is listening. The fourth stage would be silence, which is something that we cannot anticipate.

(This is a very important question. Any group leader or anyone teaching meditation needs to listen to this aspect of the teaching, which is fully explained in *Word into Silence*. They should test it against their own experience and then they will be ready to express it confidently in their own group or when teaching.)

Q. What is the relationship between meditation and social action?

A. It is a consequence of our prayer that we should be involved in the world. Every action we do should be a consequence of our prayer. In meditation we are purifying our inner life in order to go out to others. The one should flow from the other.

The end of our prayer is communion with the Body of Christ and to be in union with the Body of Christ has to be with our brothers and sisters throughout the world because that is where the resurrected Christ is present. If prayer does not help this outreach, then it is not true prayer. Love of God and love of neighbor are the essential truths and all prayer should lead us to that community that is the world. It is not just to think about it but what we can do, the thing that Christ did, since we are now in union with the liberating presence of Christ in the world.

We must be careful not to think that our meditation is a passive occupation. It is a very active act, to sit down, to practice meditation, to spend that time. Everything that it includes is active and it is about attention, not un-attention. If we really meditate, whatever we do in our life, we do it differently because we meditate. We do it with more attention, at a deeper level – with more sensitivity and compassion. It doesn't necessarily mean that we all are called to go out and do certain things that come under the umbrella of social justice. Everyone serves humanity in different ways, sometimes they may appear to be inaction but may at the same time be very deep and very meaningful.

If we are doers and we have always been doers, and are involved in social justice issues, the parish or politics, once we start meditating, we find that we are called to be very discriminating about what we do, how we spend our time. It can also lead to a deeper understanding of why we make the choices we do with regard to service.

Meditation changes our whole attitude to action. The fruits of meditation become quite apparent as you live your life. You become more compassionate, more loving, and gentler.

Q. Sometimes when you are on holiday, family members may be all together in one room and it can be difficult to get the time or quiet for meditation. Do you have any suggestions on how to handle that situation?

A. How many of us are intimidated or reluctant to say, while we are socializing or on holiday with someone, that we have to go aside to meditate. How do you approach that? Do you feel free enough to say that this is your way and for them to accept that you are not being antisocial? But that this is your discipline and you need to take the time?

We have to do what we can and not what we cannot. Not meditating should in no way be another reason to feel guilty! While strongly stressing the importance of regular meditation, John Main, was equally strong in stressing the importance of not letting meditation become another thing to feel guilty about.

If your audience is largely Roman Catholic, these are the type of questions they may well raise:

Q. Does the Church approve of meditation?

A. Yes. In the documents of Vatican Council II it is made clear that Christians are called not only to pray with others, but to "enter into their rooms to pray to their Father in secret" (Mt. 6:6); and it goes further to cite St. Paul and his exhortation that Christians "pray without ceasing" (1 Thess. 5:17). The practice of Christian meditation, faithful to the ancient tradition of the Church, is a way that fulfills the Christian prayer vocation. The Council encourages the deepening of prayer in contemplation and later documents stress the importance of recovering lost or neglected Christian traditions of contemplation.

Pope John Paul II, in November 1992, preached that "Any method of prayer is valid insofar as it is inspired by Christ and leads to Christ who is the Way, the Truth and the Life". The one who meditates enters the stream of Jesus' prayer which always flows to the Father in the power and love of the Holy Spirit.

Q. Does Christian meditation accord with the general teaching of the Church?

A. Of course. Prayer is always seen by the Church as the fount of wisdom and compassion in the Christian life.

It is a pilgrimage in faith of being wholly attentive in the presence of God. It involves leaving the self behind, going beyond ourselves to God, who is always beyond us, yet closer to us than we are to ourselves.

It is about being at prayer which is always a gift of God, not about technique.

It leads those who meditate to look for the fruit of prayer in love.

"Contemplative Christian prayer always leads to love of neighbor, to action and to the acceptance of trials, and precisely because of this it draws one close to God." from *The Letter to the Bishops of the Catholic Church on Some Aspects of Christian Meditation*, 1989, p. 18.

Q. How does this relate to the Mass/Sacraments?

A. The spiritual life, as Vatican Council II explained, is not limited to participation in the liturgy. In this light Christian meditation forms part of the whole of one's spiritual life. Meditation clearly does not replace or substitute for other forms of prayer but, by making us more aware of the centrality of the prayer of Jesus, enriches all forms.

As faithfulness to Christian meditation is of the Holy Spirit, so through the Spirit we can expect participation in the Mass and sacraments generally to be all the richer.

Q. Doesn't Meditation mean Ignatian Meditation?

A. The Spiritual Exercises of St. Ignatius (16th Century) contain certain methods of mental prayer, and since the time of their composition many religious congregations have adopted the spirituality taught and practiced by the Jesuits. The Ignatian way has come to be known and practiced as a method of "discursive meditation". Other schools of spirituality have also emerged in the life of the church, for example St. Francis de Sales in *An Introduction to the Devout Life*. St. Ignatius also, however, taught the importance of contemplation as the goal of all prayer and action.

Contemplative prayer has a long history in the Western and Eastern Churches. St. Benedict (c.480–547) has been called the Father of monasticism in the West. In writing about St. Antony (c.250–356) of Egypt, 'the father of all monks', St. Athanasius wrote that, "He prayed frequently, for he had learned that one ought to pray in secret, and pray without ceasing".

Q. What about Reason?

A. Meditation is not anti-rational. The clarity and insightfulness of reason and imagination are enhanced by the practice of meditation, (See Pope John Paul II's letter on *Faith and Reason*)

In Christian meditation the mind is alert, yet not aiming at anything other than being still and silent in God's presence. Recall the psalmist says "Be still and know that I am God". (Ps. 46)

Q. Where does it say that Jesus meditated with a mantra?

A. It doesn't. Jesus taught no "methods" of prayer but his teaching on prayer directs us to the condition of interiority, trust and simplicity. We know from Jesus' teaching on prayer that he instructs us not to "heap up empty phrases as the Gentiles do; for they think they will be heard because of their many words. Do not be like them, for your Father knows what you need before you ask him".

> "Pray then in this way:
> Our Father in heaven,
> Hallowed be your name" (Mt. 6: 7–9)

In Christian meditation there is an implicit recognition that the Father knows what we need before we ask. St. Augustine said "we say nothing that is not found in this prayer of the Lord, if we pray, properly and fittingly", and "we have Christ within us as our Teacher".

Q. Is meditation the same as contemplation?

A. Now and then we will find these words with a different meaning. However, we note that in the general introduction to *Word into Silence* John Main chooses to use the term meditation synonymously with such terms as contemplation, contemplative prayer, meditative prayer, and so on. Then he adds, "The essential context of meditation is to be found in the fundamental relationships of our lives, the relationship that we have as creatures with God, our Creator". Meditation could be said to be the work we do in faith and love to receive or enter fully into the gift of the state of contemplation already present in us through the indwelling of the Holy Spirit.

If your audience is predominantly Christian from various denominations, these are the type of questions they may well raise:

Q. Isn't this Buddhist?

A. Quite mistakenly, meditation can very easily be identified as the preserve only of the Oriental traditions, including Buddhism. Through the teaching of John Main and others in the 20th century, we have come to appreciate afresh the place of meditation in the Christian tradition.

Q. What makes meditation Christian?

A. It is our faith and love that makes meditation Christian.

With reference to St. Paul, Romans 8:26, the Spirit is pleading for us (in our inmost being beyond words, beyond thoughts, beyond images) with sighs too deep for words. The Spirit is with us in our prayer, praying within us, and as John Main tells us in *Word into Silence*, "Prayer then, is the life of the Spirit of Jesus within our human heart".

Attentiveness and receptivity are the qualities that enable us to become more completely incorporated with the Word within us, who is the Son, spoken by and returning to the Father.

Q. Does the Devil enter the empty mind?

A. In Christian meditation the work is to bring the mind and one's whole being to stillness and silence. Jesus refers to the primacy of "poverty of spirit" as the condition for entering the Kingdom of God.

The stillness of both mind and body to which the mantra guides us is a preparation for entering into our own silence, and for our progression through the spheres of silence.

Q. Where is it mentioned in Scripture?

A. Scripture provides the inspiration and purpose of all prayer. A study of the history and the tradition of the early Church will show that this way of prayer was indeed familiar to the Jewish Christians of this period.

We recall that John Cassian draws us back to the Beatitudes (Mt. 5: 1–11) arising from 'the poverty of the single verse'. He says this poverty will bring us with ready ease to the first of the beatitudes: "Blessed are the poor in spirit, for theirs is the Kingdom of Heaven". In addition, the goal Cassian proposes throughout his Conferences is purity of heart: "Blessed are the pure in heart, for they will see God".

Q. Isn't it Self-Centered?

A. No. It is all about leaving self behind and turning to the Other.

Q. Isn't it just Self-Hypnosis?

A. The mind is alert, and engaged in the art of attention. The conscious mind is never shut down but expanded beyond its habitual self-fixation.

Q. If I concentrate on the mantra am I locking out the Holy Spirit?

A. Meditation brings us to a state of open hearted receptivity to the Spirit of Jesus who dwells in our hearts. The mantra keeps us open to the Spirit in poverty and simplicity.

Q. Isn't this just Catholic?

A. Meditation becomes an expression of unity, and in a particular way for Christians. People of Christian faith can freely discover a shared faith heritage as something ancient, yet ready to come alive.

If your audience is largely secular, these are the questions they may well raise:

Q. Why do we have to bring religion into meditation?

A. Meditation purifies religion and restores it to its true purpose of teaching and inspires the spiritual unity of humanity.

Q. Do I need faith to meditate?

A. In the first place we may not be aware of what brings us to meditate. We may feel we have little or no faith.

Fidelity is needed to keep meditating.

Q. What are the physical benefits?

A. Medical evidence shows for example that meditation lowers blood pressure and enhances the immune system. But the greatest significance of meditation is enhancing the sense of our human wholeness in the harmony of body, mind and spirit.

Q. Is this the same as Centering Prayer?

A. There is an essential harmony in these two approaches to meditation. Centering Prayer places a different emphasis on the mantra.

Compiled by Desmond J. Moloney

Sharing *the* GIFT

The Role of the Christian MEDITATION Group

THE WEEKLY GROUP MEETING

The special legacy of the life and teaching of John Main is the remarkable growth of small Christian Meditation groups meeting weekly in various countries of the world. It was John Main's hope that the teaching would be shared in an organic way through small groups of men and women meeting regularly in homes, parishes, schools and work-places.

He had a profound understanding of the ancient tradition of Christians gathering to pray. As Laurence Freeman has pointed out, he saw this modern development of contemplation as originating in the communities of faith and the liturgy of the heart of the early Church. These early Christians also gathered in small groups in one another's houses. This coming together in prayer formed the 'koinonia' or the social interaction and communion that was the distinguishing mark and power of the early Church.

John Main had a clear understanding of the need of a community of faith that would solidify one's own commitment to the spiritual discipline of meditation while at the same time making the teaching available to newcomers. Our human experience tells us that meeting with others on a common pilgrimage can give us the support we need to carry on the journey. Experience has also demonstrated that when a group starts in a new geographic area, people who have never meditated before will join the group. New groups introduce new people to meditation.

There are a number of good reasons why we should meet in a meditation group once a week. Meeting in a group promotes a spiritual bond amongst the members and a mutual concern between those who have set out on a common pilgrimage. As mentioned the meditation group is really a community of faith much like the community of early Christians in St Paul's time. In commenting about meditating in a group, Fr William Johnston SJ, in his book, *The Inner Eye of Love*, says: "For example we can sit together in silent and wordless meditation. And in such a situation we can feel not only the silence in our hearts but the silence of the whole group. Sometimes such silence will be almost palpable and it can unite people more deeply than any words."

The heart of the meditation group meeting is the sharing of silence together. This is the primary reason why people around the world are spontaneously starting small groups to meditate weekly together. The power and strength of meditating together comes from the words of Jesus, "Where two or three are gathered in my name there I am in the midst of them" (Matt

18:20). This is the primary reason for getting together once a week. It is as if the meditators instinctively realize that this is a journey that is difficult to make alone; it is a journey that is so much easier if we make it with others. It is true that no one else can meditate for us, that we meditate in solitude every day, but at the same time we realize that we need the support of others if we are to persevere on this journey.

The group setting enables beginners to learn 'how' to meditate. Newcomers can be integrated into a group at any point in time. In addition the weekly group meeting provides support and encouragement to those who might be discouraged or experiencing difficulties 'on the path'. All of us need from time to time, the encouragement of seeing others who are faithful and committed to the discipline.

We also need to absorb the teaching more deeply and we do so at the weekly meeting with the playing of a recorded talk by John Main. There are now about 200 talks by Father John available on various aspects of meditation. These talks give instruction and deepen motivation and so help us to persevere on the path. They give us a spiritual boost each week: part of the food we need for the journey.

THE ROLE OF THE CHRISTIAN MEDITATION GROUP

The weekly Christian Meditation group is a significant phenomenon in the church today. It is part of the great movement of the Holy Spirit that is deepening the spiritual life of lay Christians all over the world. Groups now meet in over 100 countries, in parishes, homes, offices, schools, prisons, hospitals and communities.

The meditation group is different from the ordinary prayer group. Although meditation does not exclude other forms of prayer it is, for meditators, the foundation of their spiritual life. Therefore the weekly meditation group does not focus on vocal prayer, petition or praise. This should be made clear to newcomers.

The format of the group is simple and the meeting is usually shorter that a prayer group – about one hour. It consists of three essential elements:

- time for the teaching (a recording or talk)
- half-hour of meditation in silence
- time for questions or sharing

The group leader accepts the responsibility on behalf of the group to keep to this format. The leader therefore arranges for the recording to be played at the beginning of the group, time the meditation and guide the question/sharing time.

The group is a community. It is bonded by a deepening spiritual friendship among its members. It encourages people to persevere in meditation, support their daily practice and helps people to get started again when they give up. The group is also a centre of spiritual hospitality for anyone seeking God. It is a teaching group where people can learn about meditation in the Christian faith and be helped to start.

The leader of the group is an ordinary meditator like anyone else. He or she is not set up as a guru or an expert. But they do share their faith and commitment. After meditating for a while they can probably respond to the simple questions of beginners from their own experience.

Group leaders, though, also belong to a wider community and can turn to others for help and advice at any time. They are able to deepen their own understanding of meditation continually by reading John Main or Laurence Freeman or listening to their recordings, by attending retreats or seminars, and of course by their own ongoing reading of scripture and through their sacramental life.

Summary of talk by Laurence Freeman OSB in Singapore

THE CHRISTIAN MEDITATION GROUP LEADER

The qualities of a group leader:

- A personal commitment to meditation as taught in the Christian Meditation Community
- The wish to share this gift with others.
- A sense of belonging to The World Community for Christian Meditation which this teaching has created around the world.

The responsibilities of a group leader:

- To be a stable center for the group's weekly meeting. To be there or arrange for the group to be led by another. To arrange the practical aspects of time and space for the meeting. To have the recording or talk prepared and to time the meditation.
- To welcome newcomers and introduce them to the teaching and to the other members of the group in a friendly way. To show an interest in the newcomer's questions and progress.
- To encourage the daily practice of the twice-daily commitment to meditation but also recognize that it takes people time to build up this discipline.
- To be the contact person to the wider community of meditators, locally and globally.

Challenges of leading a group:

- To see that the meaning and strength of the group is found in its faith not its numbers. A group of 2 or 3 is as good as a group of 20 or 30.
- To see that people may come to the group for a while and then move on. You cannot tell what the Spirit may have done in that person through their short stay in the group.
- To deepen your own personal practice of meditation in order to be better present for others.
- To see that your experience of God is deepened by being part of the way that others come to know God.

Summary of talk by Laurence Freeman OSB in Singapore

Excellent Resource: *A Pearl of Great Price – Sharing the Gift of Meditation*
Laurence Freeman OSB

JOHN MAIN'S DEEP INSIGHT ABOUT SMALL GROUPS

It has been said that in each age God raises up prophets and teachers to ensure His work is carried on. John Main is certainly regarded as one of these great spiritual teachers of the 20th century. But he was also in a real sense a prophet. John Main had a deep insight and prophetic vision that his teaching on silence and stillness in prayer would be primarily handed down in small groups. It was his hope that this teaching and practice would be shared in an organic way through support groups of men and women meeting on a weekly basis in homes, churches, schools and work places. He had a profound understanding of the ancient tradition of Christians gathering together to pray.

MEDITATION GROUPS: COMMUNITIES OF FAITH

As Laurence Freeman has pointed out, "John Main saw this modern development of contemplation as originating in the communities of faith and the liturgy at the heart of the early church. These early Christians also gathered in small groups in one another's houses. This coming together in prayer formed the "koinonia", or the social interaction and communion, that was the distinguishing mark and power of the early church". These small groups met to pray and offer support and encouragement to each other in their common faith.

THE HISTORICAL ROOTS OF SMALL GROUPS

There is no doubt that the teaching of spirituality is historically rooted in the tradition of the small group. The Israelites were divided up into small tribes and close family units, particularly during their sojourn in the wilderness. Jesus chose a small group of twelve to form the heart of his ministry. Throughout the last 2,000 years small groups of men and women have banded together in the monastic life to live in community and support each other on the spiritual journey. It seems only natural that people who are praying contemplatively in the 21st century should also come together in groups to support each other on their common pilgrimage.

SMALL GROUPS ARE TODAY REDEFINING SPIRITUALITY

A recent book *Sharing the Journey* by Robert Wuthnow documents the growing popularity and influence of small groups in creating community and teaching spirituality. Wuthnow maintains small groups "may be redefining spirituality" and that the church is once again becoming alive in the humble homes of those on the spiritual path. The author also confirms through research that small groups have emerged in response to the impersonalization of society and the weakening of family and community ties.

What has experience taught us over the years since John Main started the first Christian Meditation group at Ealing Abbey in London in 1975. Here is what we have learned about the role of the weekly meditation group.

WHY MEDITATORS MEET IN GROUPS

The heart of the meditation group is the sharing of silence together. This is the primary reason why, spontaneously, people around the world are starting small groups to meditate weekly together. The power and strength of meditation together comes from the words of Jesus, "Where two or three are gathered in my name, there I am in the midst of them" (Matthew 18:2).

This is the foremost reason for getting together once a week. It is as if meditators instinctively realize that this is a journey that is difficult to make alone; it is a journey that is so much easier if we make it with others. It is true that no one else can meditate for us, that we meditate by ourselves each day, but at the same time, we realize that we need the support of others if we are to persevere on this journey.

THE DEVELOPMENT OF A SPIRITUAL BOND AMONG MEMBERS OF THE GROUP

Meeting in a group promotes a spiritual bond amongst the members and a mutual concern between those who have set out on a common pilgrimage. The meditation group is really a community of faith, much as the early Christians experienced community in St. Paul's time.

The group setting enables beginners to learn how to meditate. Newcomers can be integrated into a group at any point in time. Experience has shown that when a group starts in a new geographic area, people who have never meditated before will join the group. New groups introduce new meditators to the teaching.

SMALL GROUPS GIVE SUPPORT AND ENCOURAGEMENT ON THE SPIRITUAL PATH

The weekly group meeting provides support and encouragement to those who might be discouraged or experiencing difficulties "on the path". All of us need, from time to time, the encouragement of seeing others faithful and committed to the discipline.

We also need to absorb the teaching more deeply and we do so at the weekly meeting with the playing of a taped talk by John Main on some aspect of Christian Meditation. There are now 250 talks by Father John and additional talks by Laurence Freeman available on various aspects of meditation. These talks give instruction, deepen our motivation, and help us to persevere on the path. They give us a spiritual boost each week: part of the food we need for the journey.

The question answer period at the end of the meeting often help immeasurably in clarifying situations, not only for the questioner who is often a newcomer but also for other members of the group. Discussion allows members to express their doubts, fears and misunderstandings of the teaching.

WHERE DO GROUPS MEET?

Groups meet in diverse locations and at various hours through-out the day and evening. There are now over 1,200 groups worldwide meeting in 60 countries of the world in homes, apartments, schools, churches, rectories, religious communities, Christian Meditation centers, chapels, universities, prisons, government office buildings, a department store, senior citizens' homes and factories.

Lists of groups and times of meetings are available from Christian Meditation group leaders in various countries. An inter-national list of groups is available from The International Centre, The World Community for Christian Meditation, St. Mark's Church, Myddelton Square, London ECR1XX, England.

WHAT HAPPENS AT THE WEEKLY MEETING?

The typical weekly group meeting lasts about one hour and includes an opening welcome to the members by the group leader. Most groups light a candle symbolic of the presence of Christ. This is followed by the playing of a 15 minute cassette tape by John Main or Laurence Freeman on some aspect of the practice and teaching of meditation, followed by the heart of the meeting, 25 minutes of silent meditation. At the conclusion of meditation any announcements can be made and newcomers given a chance to ask any questions pertaining to the teaching. In more and more groups the meditation group leader is giving a short five minute talk relating to John Main's talk that evening. The group leader then asks for dialogue from the participants on the points he/she has made.

ON STARTING A GROUP

How do groups start? The most important ingredient in starting a new group is the commitment of a leader to the time and effort required to set up and guide a group. A decision must be made about the time and evening of the meeting and a location must be found (a quiet location if possible). A number of things can be done to attract newcomers to the group. A letter can be sent to all churches in the area asking for pulpit and bulletin announcements about the establishment of the group. Posters can also be produced for church bulletin boards. Notices can be sent to religious/ daily/weekly or community newspapers. An announcement can be sent to local cablevision TV stations and radio stations. Notices can be pinned on shopping plaza bulletin boards.

THE ROLE OF THE GROUP LEADER

The leader must work in setting up the group as if humanely speaking everything depended on himself/herself, while at the same time realizing that in the dimension of faith the growth and success of the group will depend on God. *Numbers* are unimportant in a group. Our Lord said "where two or three are gathered in my name there I am in the midst of them". Where two meditators are gathered there is a meditation group. Once a group starts, others will join in time.

A leader will require a tape recorder, some of John Main's/Laurence Freeman's cassette tapes on meditation, and a timer. Where electricity or a tape recorder is not available selections can be read from books by John Main or Laurence Freeman. Many group leaders utilize a pre-programmed cassette timing tape with a few moments of music, 25 minutes of silence and music that signals the end of the meditation period. But more than these material items the meditation leader will require faith and commitment. Faith to "wait on the Lord" not only in meditation but also for the increase in new members. But God works through the instrumentality of human beings. If the leader has worked to communicate information about the new group, God will bring the increase ... and a new meditation group will be born and will flourish.

WHAT ARE THE OTHER ADVANTAGES OF SMALL GROUPS

Small Christian Meditation groups have a great advantage in adapting to their environment. They require virtually no resources, other than the time their members devote to the group each week.

The small group provides a sense of community for people who feel the loss and breakdown of neighborhoods and personal family ties. The need for encouragement, support and sharing are additional reasons for joining a group.

We all need the affirmation of others and thus our faith can be strengthened through the bonds of love, caring and fellowship that develop in the small group. Basic spiritual and human values are shared in a group setting and subsequent friendships develop.

We are not, contrary to public perception, a society of rugged individualists, who wish to go it entirely alone, but rather we are a communal people, capable of banding together in bands of mutual support.

THE SPIRITUAL REVOLUTION TAKING PLACE TODAY WITHIN SMALL GROUPS

While these findings will be of interest to anyone participating in Christian Meditation groups, either as members or leaders, it should be pointed out that the period of meditation itself will provide a strong bond of unity within the group. Because it is the prayer of Jesus Himself, it necessarily follows that a spirit of love and friendship should develop within the group.

As Laurence Freeman has written: "The early Christians experienced this inner reality of prayer and knew the strong bond of unity it gave. But as the church grew older, its emphasis fell more and more upon formal prayer and external observance. Its interiority weakened, and wherever it weakened, the church's influence diminished and her spiritual life grew more sterile".

Today in the small group setting we are recapturing a prayer that leads us from the head to the heart, from fragmentation to unity, from isolation to caring. This *is* the spiritual revolution taking place around the world today.

Paul Harris

RESOURCES

THE WORLD COMMUNITY FOR CHRISTIAN MEDITATION

The School of Meditation

Primary Resources for Beginners in Meditation and for New Groups

INDIVIDUALS JUST BEGINNING TO MEDITATE

Individuals need to feel personal support. The group leader should offer to meet personally with a new meditator to discuss the practice and respond to questions. If the beginner cannot attend a group regularly some other way of staying in touch should be suggested – the local monthly meeting or some other form of personal support.

BOOKS

- *Christian Meditation: Your Daily Practice* – Laurence Freeman
- *The Inner Pilgrimage* – Laurence Freeman
- *Christian Meditation: The Gethsemane Talks* – John Main
- *Light Within* – Laurence Freeman
- *Moment of Christ* – John Main
- *Silence and Stillness in Every Season: Daily Readings* with John Main

CDs

- *In the Beginning* – John Main
- *The Essential Teaching* – John Main
- *The Essentials of Christian Meditation* – Laurence Freeman
- *Letting Go* – Laurence Freeman

DVDs

- YouTube clips (www.youtube.com/user/meditatiowccm)

WEB

www.wccm.org and The School of Meditation webpages (icon The School)

- Weekly Teachings
- Weekly Readings

NEW GROUPS

Like individuals, new groups need personal support. The group leader should feel connected regularly to the local or regional or national coordinator. They should be encouraged to do the Essential Teaching Weekend and to use the Weekly Teachings in their weekly groups, copying it for their members if possible as lectio during the week. The group leader should be helped to become familiar with *The Pearl of Great Price* and be helped to understand the format of our groups and the need for consistency. They should also be helped how to select and prioritise the resources listed below, eg a new group in its early days should concentrate on the elements of the basic teaching before moving into use of the Meditatio CDs.

BOOKS

- *The Hunger for Depth and Meaning* – John Main (ed. Peter Ng)
- *Word into Silence* – John Main
- *Silence and Stillness in Every Season: Daily Readings* with John Main
- *Selfless Self* – Laurence Freeman
- *Essential Writings* – John Main (Orbis)

CDs

- *TimePeace* (MedioMedia)
- *In the Beginning and other Communitas Series* – John Main
- *Lord Teach us to Pray* – Laurence Freeman
- *Practical Wisdom (3 series)* – Laurence Freeman

DVDs

- *The Pilgrimage* (Medio Media)
- *The Journey of Meditation* – Laurence Freeman

WEB

www.wccm.org and The School of Meditation webpages (icon The School)

- Weekly Teachings
- Weekly Readings

If you wish to find out more about these resources please contact your WCCM national Coordinator or email welcome@wccm.org.

* * *

Visit the website www.TheSchoolofMeditatio.org for information about new resources or contact the International Coordinator by email: SchoolCoordinator.org